FLOWER MAGIC
of the DRUIDS

"*Flower Magic of the Druids* is a lovely book that offers instruction on how to infuse and extract herbal preparations in harmony with the seasons to energetically capture the subtle essences of individual flowers and other plant portions to enhance love, protection, and good fortune. *Flower Magic of the Druids* is a reminder that the power of nature with intention can be a tool for transformation."

BRIGITTE MARS,
AUTHOR OF *THE SEXUAL HERBAL*

FLOWER MAGIC
of the DRUIDS

How to Craft Potions, Spells, and Enchantments

JON G. HUGHES

Destiny Books

Rochester, Vermont

Destiny Books
One Park Street
Rochester, Vermont 05767
www.DestinyBooks.com

Text stock is SFI certified

Destiny Books is a division of Inner Traditions International

Cataloging-in-Publication Data for this title is available from the Library of Congress

ISBN 978-1-64411-639-5 (print)
ISBN 978-1-64411-640-1 (ebook)

Printed and bound in the United States by Lake Book Manufacturing, LLC
The text stock is SFI certified. The Sustainable Forestry Initiative® program
promotes sustainable forest management.

10 9 8 7 6 5 4 3 2 1

Text design and layout by Priscilla Harris Baker
This book was typeset in Garamond Premier Pro with Acherus Grotesque, Gill
Sans, Futura, Legacy Sans, and Serat used as display typefaces

To send correspondence to the author of this book, mail a first-class letter to the
author c/o Inner Traditions • Bear & Company, One Park Street, Rochester, VT
05767, and we will forward the communication, or contact the author directly at
jongarstanhughes@gmail.com.

Contents

PART 3

The Druid's Garden

The Wonders That Surround Us

From the very first moment that humanity became aware of our natural environment and the wonders that surround us, flowers have played a prominent role in our existence. From the practical elements of survival to inspiring our various burgeoning belief systems, from early primitive art to classical literature, wherever we look, flowers appear in every aspect of our lives and cultural development.

Within the Druidic lore that I grew up with in Wales, flowers were everywhere—in the wild wood, in our pastures and meadows, in our gardens and homes, and especially within the dark, smoke-filled workshops of the learned Druids who were responsible for my training. The ubiquitous presence of flowers is due in no small part to the insights of our pre-Celtic ancestors who, thousands of years before the arrival of the Celtic influence on our shores, developed a system of flower magic that is as relevant today as it was during the ancient megalithic era of stone circles and ritual standing stones. Over time, this original fascination with the beautiful appearance and fragrance of our wildflowers developed into a sophisticated lore of magic that embraces all the many aspects of our native flora. It is not surprising that this delicate and precise magic tradition has often mistakenly been associated solely with female Druids, though it would be wrong to suggest that the delicate nature of the flower in any way reduces the potency of its magic powers any more than the workings of female Druids are lesser in any way than those of their male counterparts. The history of the tradition tells us that both male and female Druids have used this unique magic practice with equal effect and, with correct application, will continue to do so long into the future.

Today we can benefit from the millennia of exploration and experimentation of our ancestors by utilizing the flower magic of the Welsh Druidic tradition that has been handed down to us. Many of the flowering plants that grew and continue to grow in the Welsh countryside continue to be foraged by practitioners of Druidic lore, and many have found new homes in physic gardens—botanical gardens that cultivate and display medicinal plants. Over the thousands of years since the magical benefits of flowers have been recognized, we have continued to forage vital flowers from our meadows, hedgerows, fields, and forests in order to extract the cardinal essences essential to the magical lore of our forefathers and foremothers. These ancient cunning folk, Druids, witches, and forest conjurers all understood the benefits of each individual plant and its flowers and were the source of an arcane lore that informed the miceiners, wort doctors, alchemists, and apothecaries that evolved into the present-day physicians, pharmacists, and chemists of mainstream medicine as well as the homeopaths, herbalists, and complementary healers that practice beside them.

Nicholas Culpeper (1616–1654), the most famous of these herbal practitioners, recognized the unique gifts of flowers among his voluminous herbarium, stating that "the best way of preserving the excellent virtues of flowers is by keeping them conserved," underscoring the Druidic lore of conservation and regeneration. Another prominent British alternative herbal practitioner, Edward Bach (1886–1936), utilized many of the same native flowers in his original collection of Bach flower remedies, inspired by his connection to the same Welsh flower lore, which he adapted to classical homeopathic traditions. Bach, born of Welsh parents, returned to North Wales to look for inspiration for his flower remedies from the long-standing local Welsh tradition. He began by appropriating the Druidic practice of gathering the dew from the petals of flowers in the belief that the early morning dew had absorbed the virtues and attributes of the flower on which it had settled. While Bach was keen to appropriate the idea of flower magic and healing, he failed to grasp the basic tenets of the Druidic lore he encountered. As we will see, the process is far more complex and subtle than he understood, depending as it does on more than one individual essence from each flower to achieve its aims.

Both Culpeper and Bach also declined to include one of the most important elements of the use and conservation of the wildflowers they employed in their work—that of the role of the humble yet indispensable honeybee, the proud pollinators of the wildflowers of the British Isles. They are our most prolific pollinators, and much of our produce is dependent upon their efforts. We should never underestimate the value of our industrious honeybees and the contribution they make to our society and our spiritual lore. These ubiquitous picnic invaders are the powerhouse of Druidic flower magic, not only pollinating over 80 percent of our wildflowers, but also providing us with magnificent wild honey and beeswax, both vital components of flower magic. We are also indebted to these fascinating creatures not only for these invaluable physical gifts but also for the knowledge we have gained from observing how they govern their communities and the physical structure of their honeycombs, which are built with individual cell structures in hexagonal form, a shape that informs the very core beliefs of Druidic lore. It is not possible to look at the use of flowers in any magic tradition without also considering the indispensable symbiotic relationship between the flower and the bee, and as we explore the structure and community of the bee colony, we discover the contributions the bee makes to both the basic physical and spiritual aspects of Druidic flower magic.

During our exploration of this unique magic practice, we will look at the doctrine that underpins Druidic flower magic and its application, together with the range of flowering botanicals it employs, and the techniques used in gathering the various flowers used in crafting its potions and philters. We will look at how single flowers are used in the extraction of the potent cardinal essences that become the basis of the many powerful potions used in this magic tradition and the ancient rituals used in creating and empowering them.

It is, however, important to recognize that the Druidic lore we are about to explore is just one of many traditions that may be found around the British Isles. Through years of research, study, and enquiry, I have discovered that though many of these traditions may vary in detail, they have much more in common than that which separates them, and it is often easy to see how some of these variations have evolved while still sharing the same origins.

Our journey of discovery concludes with a detailed listing of the many plants, trees, and briars native to the British Isles, as well as Europe and Eurasia, used in the tradition, with information on their virtues and attributes, their flowering months, and other aspects of their use and conservation, providing a comprehensive and practical workbook for anyone intending to develop their interest in Druidic flower magic.

The tradition we are about to investigate is one that evolved over millennia in rural Wales, in a specific region of South Wales that incorporates the South Wales Valleys and extends into the historic Welsh Marches, the borderland between the ancient principality of Wales and what was then Norman England, an area that still remains unique within the British Isles to the present day. Nonetheless, nearly all the botanicals detailed within the text can be found growing wild in Europe, particularly in Northern and Western Europe; only a few grow just in the British Isles, such as navelwort, round-leaved crowfoot, western sea lavender, and wild clary. Of the 149 species listed in the directory in chapter 10, only about 30 cannot be found anywhere in North America. Many of these plants have been introduced to North America and have become naturalized, some adapting so well that they have become invasive. Quite a few are native to North America, among them yarrow (*Achillea millefolium*), marsh marigold (*Caltha palustris*), and juniper (*Juniperus communis*), or are very common and readily identified, such as buttercup, dandelion, and goldenrod. Others listed in the directory have related North American species, such as *Solanum americanum* (American black nightshade), *Sorbus americana* (American mountain ash or rowan), and *Fragaria virginiana* (Virginia or wild strawberry). However, beyond the availability of specific species, the overarching doctrine of the three cardinals and the methods of extracting, refining, and reuniting them is valid for all flowers, whether listed in the directory or not, and if the reader can identify suitable local flowers with appropriate virtues that may be harvested without jeopardizing their sustainability, then the reader can undertake the workings that follow with every expectation of success.

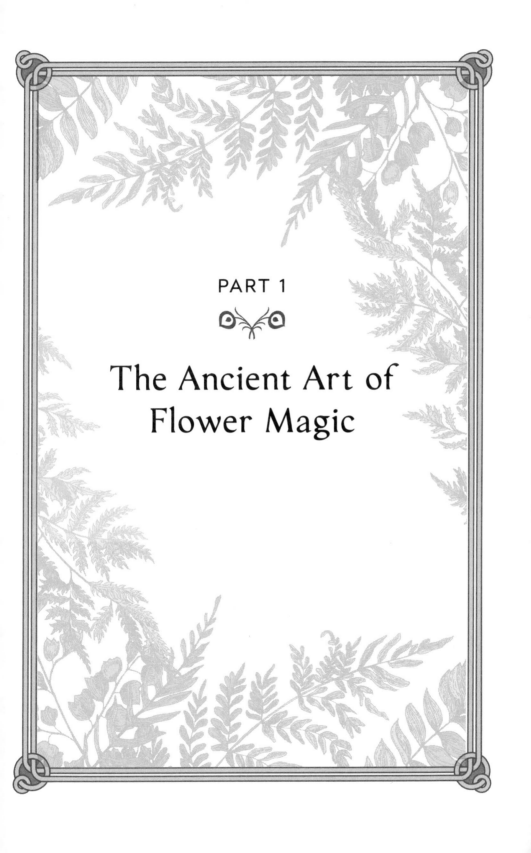

PART 1

The Ancient Art of Flower Magic

ONE

Origins of Druidic Flower Magic

Throughout the history of humankind, no matter where they may be located around the world, flowers have played a vital role in our society, culture, and belief systems. We appreciate not only their unfettered beauty, wonderful fragrance, and potent physical properties but also readily acknowledge the positive effect they have upon our feelings of well-being, their appeal to our aesthetic pleasure, and the strong cultural and religious significance that has developed whenever and wherever they appear.

If we examine the many and various belief systems that every civilization around the globe has created throughout history, we will see the ubiquitous presence of flowers and their use in a bewildering variety of ways—not only for their aesthetic beauty but also their supranatural properties. As well as being used to decorate altars, shrines, temples, and other places of worship in virtually every culture, old and new, flowers have earned themselves a formidable reputation as magical devices, and it is here that we direct the following chapters.

Many ancient belief systems have employed flowers in their magic rituals, often as the primary focus of their workings. In the ancient Druidic lore that we are exploring, the use of flowers as a magic device is so central to the wider lore that it has earned a special branch of magic workings unto itself. This flower magic extends right back to the arcane workings of the old lore and still occupies a prominent position in modern craft lore. It would be a mistake to assign this tradition to the Celtic influence, which arrived on the shores of Great Britain and Ireland millennia after this lore was developed. In the same way, it is foolish to assign the great majority of ancient Druidic lore to any other source than the Welsh, Scottish, Irish, and early Britons. The Celts, or the Gauls or Gaels as they called themselves, arrived on the islands thousands of years after the height of the Druidic culture, long after the building of the monumental stone circles and the other monolithic sites that are scattered over the length and breadth of the British Isles.

It is reasonable to assume that the presence of flowers in the Druidic lore of Wales is as old as any that may be found elsewhere, predating the arrival of the Gaelic (Celtic) influence in the region by several millennia; while it may be said that the Gaelic influence indeed affected the indigenous art and culture of the Welsh, it had very little, if any, influence on Druidic beliefs or teachings, including that of flower magic. A number of parables within the Druidic teachings tell us of the arrival of the strange and unfamiliar Gaelic beliefs from across the southern waters and modern archaeology confirms the rapid changes to the artistic representations and beliefs of the native Welsh population. But other than the introduction of the title of Druid to the leaders of the long-established learned class of the local tribes, neither modern-day scholars nor the ancient lore of the Welsh Druids acknowledge any changes or additions to the original beliefs of the Welsh Druids as a result of the arrival of the Gaelic influence upon our shores.

THE EARLY DRUIDS

We cannot say exactly when the cunning folk of Wales, Scotland, and Ireland began gathering the roots and seeds of the plants they used on a regular basis and replanting them in their gardens and enclosures, but it is to these ingenious cultivators that we owe much of our early understanding of medicinal, culinary, and spiritual plants. We have ample archaeological evidence showing that our hunter-gatherer nomadic ancestors foraged plants for food and other uses, and it is broadly believed that it was at this time that we became aware of the subtler benefits of the plants of the forests and meadows of the British Isles.

Our current understanding is that the art of flower magic, along with many other Druidic traditions, began at a time soon after the retreat of the ice fields of the Last Glacial Maximum, some 12,000 to 25,000 years ago, as the populations of the British Isles began to return to their homelands and resettle in the ancient lands of their ancestors. The first physical evidence of the practice may be seen in the recovered artifacts of the settlements of the Grooved ware people, some five thousand years before the building of the Egyptian pyramids, and our inherited tradition tells us that many of these original workings continue to the present day.

When these nomadic hunter-gatherer folk gave up following the herds of wild animals and began to settle in extended family groups and to build more permanent homes, we see the emergence of the first specializations in these tribal groups, with individuals focusing on specific skills and trades rather than doing everything that their smaller families needed to survive. Some individuals discovered skills in pottery because others chose to become farmers and growers and relieved them of their need to grow crops and tend cattle. They became the first potters, eventually bartering their pots for grain and meat with their neighbors and clansmen. Other individuals chose to be carpenters. The word *carpenter* originates, in part, from the Old Celtic word *carpentom,* meaning a "small wagon." These carts were made from wood, therefore someone who makes things from wood became known as a carpenter. Others built rude huts from daube and wattle (mud and hay), and yet others wove the coarse cloth from which their clothes were fashioned. Each traded their goods, skills, and time with the others, and all benefited from the development of what was to become the model for all village life. Some devoted themselves to defending the homes, crops, and livestock of their tribe, and we see here the beginning of what were to become the tribal armies of the clans, providing protection and security to the tribe as it grew in size and became self-sustaining, each tribe with its collection of skilled craftsmen and women.

With this hard-earned security and the predictability of their cultivated crops providing the group with year-round food and drink, it is understandable that some within the tribe turned their thoughts and attention to the more spiritual side of life; it is these individuals who, through their careful observation of nature and their experimentation with botanicals, found more to life than simple existence. These learned individuals soon gained respect within the tribe due to their ability to predict the changes in the weather and the passing of the seasons, allowing the farmers to plan the growing, harvesting, and storing of their crops and the cattle breeders to predict the breeding cycles of their herds. By closely observing how wild animals behaved when they were sick or wounded, these wise men and women began to use familiar herbs, barks, flowers, and roots in a similar way to treat their clans folk. By observing the movement of the sun, moon, and planets, they could foretell the passing of time together with the changing of the seasons and began recording the progress of the planets by aligning markers with prominent features on the horizon, which in time developed into the monolithic stone circles they left as their legacy. Over time and as a result of their universal knowledge and wisdom, these learned men and women were elevated to the high tables of their chieftains and princes, gaining a reputation for wisdom, cunning, and spiritual insight that extended all across Europe. Around three thousand years later, the Gauls arrived on the British Isles and gave these learned men and women a name derived from their Celtic language, and from that time, they became known as Druids. By the time the invading Roman armies arrived, the Druids enjoyed a formidable reputation as military strategists and ferocious fighters well as the possessors of the ancient lore of the Isles of Britain.

At some point, these learned individuals began replanting the roots and seeds—not of edible crops, but of the precious herbs they needed for their magic workings and remedies—and as they did, so did the cunning folk and wisewomen who lived in the burgeoning villages and hamlets that began to establish themselves in the landscape of the Isles of Britain.

ARRIVAL AND INFLUENCE OF CHRISTIANITY

When Christianity began to strengthen its grip on the population and the early saints built their churches and monasteries, it is not surprising that people began to turn to the Christian clergy and monks to heal their ills and protect their homes. Many of these early converts were pagans and some were notable Druids, encouraged to embrace the new Christian religion by being canonized as saints upon their conversion. This became such a common practice that this period, between the fifth and sixth centuries, became known as the Age of the Saints in Wales, the traditional home of the majority of the Druids of Britain.

Initially, as a response to the needs of their parishioners, these early monks took with them their knowledge and experience in the indigenous healing plants and established their own medicinal gardens, crafting traditional remedies by copying the old ways, substituting the pagan spells and incantations that always accompanied earlier cures with Christian prayer, invoking God's assistance in curing the patient. Later, during the period now known as the Dark Ages, Christian monk-healers abandoned the use of herbal remedies, calling the use of mundane herbs and other cures pagan and anti-Christian: only God would decide who was cured and only he would decide who was to live or die. All that was needed for an effective cure was prayer and devotion; everything else was heathen, ineffective, and unnecessary.

It was not until centuries later that the church once again accepted the efficacy of herbal and other medicinal cures, reinstating many of the abandoned physic gardens and herbaria of the monasteries and reintroducing the remedies and plants that had been in continuous use in the gardens of many wisewomen, Druids, and cunning folk outside their monastery walls.

These same flowers and herbs formed the basis of many of the medical advances of the following centuries, reinforced by their uninterrupted use by the folk magic practitioners throughout the British Isles. The hiatus in herbal medicine created by the Dark Ages had little to no effect upon the use of indigenous flowers by the Druids in their flower magic potions and philters.

Virtually every species of indigenous flower has its place in Druidic flower magic, many also contributing their leaves, roots, seeds, and stalks to the practical workings of Druidic lore. It is believed that the Druids may well have been one of the very first cultures to discover the spiritual powers of flowers but were, and still are, not the only belief system to recognize this vital spiritual resource. Exploring some of these other cultures will aid our understanding of these spiritual essences and how they may be used.

TWO

Other Flower Traditions and Practices

The ancient art of flower magic has been passed from generation to generation through the learned class of Druids, which spans the eons and still remains a vital and potent practice to the present day. At the same time the Druids were practicing this vibrant art, other cultures around the world were developing their own systems of flower magic.

Both the Chinese and Indian cultures had a sophisticated flower magic tradition, as well as utilizing a vast array of flowers in their medicinal repertoires. Flowers may be found in magic cultures as diverse as the Scandinavians, the peoples of the antipodes, and the Native Americans. Practically every ancient civilization, north and south, east and west, had their own flower magic, and many still remain in practice to this day. No matter which ancient culture we examine—Egyptian, Roman, Greek, or any of the diverse cultures of Asia—flowers have been used to symbolize sentiments, emotions, and magical potency in folklore, mythology, literature, and theater ranging from the classical plays of the ancient Greeks to the ageless puppetry and poetry of Chinese culture.

The aesthetic beauty of flowers is undeniable and has been recognized in every culture since time immemorial. Frequently used purely as a decorative accessory, flowers have also been used for their wonderful aromas, which have long been considered beneficial to the body and spirit, and it is here that we see the ancient beginnings of what we now call aromatherapy. Each flower has a distinctive and unique fragrance, which has, throughout history, defined the popularity and social significance of flowers. Most readers will have their own favorites and would be more than capable of distinguishing between roses and lavender, lilies and honeysuckle, and many others. Because of the unique nature of each species and the emotions and memories that their appearance and fragrance invoke in most people, it became a common practice to attribute many of the most prolific and popular species with particular symbolism and even a specific form of social meaning.

MEDIEVAL FLOWER TRADITIONS

In the later medieval period, small flower bouquets were given as gifts and garlands of fresh flowers were worn around the body or upon the head both as a form of decoration at festivals and to portray meanings and sentiments at auspicious gatherings or on significant days of the pagan or Christian year. Fresh flowers were also used for protection. When Europe was gripped by the plague or Black Death, posies or nosegays of fresh flowers were worn or carried to protect the wearer from the deadly illness. During the same period, homes, churches, and other places of gathering also used displays of fresh flowers and pomanders containing fresh flower petals for protection, in the belief that their presence would act as an apotropaic device. These widely held beliefs found their way into the folklore of the day, and many still remain. Children sing the playground rhyme "Ring around the rosie, a pocket full of posies" without even thinking of its origin as protection against the bubonic plague. Likewise, wedding guests throw flower petals on newly married couples to grant them fertility, and participants in fairs and festivals adorn themselves with fresh flowers, forgetting that, as well as being decorative, they were originally worn to disguise the wearer so that daemons and fairies would not recognize them and drag them off to their secret realms.

THE LANGUAGE OF FLOWERS

Much later in the history of the British Isles, during the reign of Queen Victoria (1837–1901), carrying flower posies once again became popular, only then as fashion accessories. All sorts of decorative flower holders were devised in silver, gold, and other elaborate jewelry forms and pinned to the lapels of fashionable ladies and gentlemen. More traditional paper or lace doilies were used to secure the small bouquets and were frequently fastened to the wearer's bodice or waist, while hair garlands became the most popular form of headwear at weddings.

The newly invented term *tussie-mussie* entered the vocabulary to describe these popular accessories, and a whole "language of flowers" evolved from this new interest, giving each flower a specific symbolic meaning. A tussie-mussie, which was a small bouquet, was assembled from flowers, each of which had a separate meaning that together conveyed a specific message to the recipient of the bouquet; this floral code, when read as a whole, communicated a complex meaning in the same way that a series of words can, when combined, make a meaningful sentence. This flower language rapidly expanded to prescribe special secret meanings to the way flowers were given and received: those offered with the right hand were given in agreement to a special question, while those given with the left hand represented a firm no. If the bouquet was proffered upside down, then the meaning of the flowers was reversed, and if the bouquet was offered with the stems pointing toward the person next to the recipient, then the message they contained was meant for that person and not the recipient. As this flower language became more and more complex, no household of standing would be without one of the many popular books on the subject, and no conversation at a ladies' afternoon tea would be complete without some mention of the secret language of flowers, which, of course, was no secret to anyone.

These elaborate and weighty flower language books contained detailed descriptions of both the meaning of each individual flower species and exactly how the complicated tussie-mussie could be assembled, along with instructions on the equally complex meanings attributed to the giving and receiving of the assembled bouquets.

Victorian Flower Language and the Druidic Tradition

If we look carefully at the specific meanings assigned to each flower species by these inventive Victorian authors, we cannot fail to see a strong correspondence to the much older tradition of the flower magic of the ancient Druids of the British Isles, and it is not unreasonable to conclude that elements of this much older tradition had survived via the cunning folk, wisewomen, and Druids, having been handed down from generation to generation.

Flower (Common Name)	Flower Language Meaning	Druidic Flower Attributes
Anemone	Forsaken	Dispels unwanted affection
Angelica	Inspiration	Develops creativity
Apple blossom	Preference	Identifies hidden love
Belladonna (deadly nightshade)	Silence	Bonds secret intentions
Bluebell	Humility	Binds purity and honor
Borage	Bluntness	Provides powerful protection
Chamomile	Patience	Encourages peace, contentment
Clover	Think of me	Creates a powerful bond
Daffodil	Regard	Banishes worries, lifts anxieties
Daisy	Innocence, loyalty	Attracts love and affection
Forget-me-not	Do not forget me	Binds people through love
Honeysuckle	Binding love	Binds lifelong love
Iris	Wisdom, trust	Develops and amplifies wisdom
Lavender	Distrust	Identifies infidelity
Lily, white water	Virginity, purity	Guards against impurity
Marigold	Jealousy, grief	Imbues joy and happiness
Mint	Virtue	Cleanses and purifies
Rose, red	Love	Binds love, increases lust
Rose, white	Innocence	Attracts young love, purity
Rosemary	Remembrance	Tests endurance and affection
Violet	Modesty, trust	Binds virginity, imbues patience

The preceding table provides a brief comparison of a small selection of the many flowers used in both traditions, comparing the meanings and attributes assigned to each. The entire subject would benefit from a serious and detailed study that goes beyond the purview of this exploration.

We can already see two potential contradictions from the above comparison. The first being that although the attributes assigned to some flowers are similar in both traditions, in the majority of examples they differ significantly. Here we see the difficulty in differentiating between the cultural meanings, with specific species representing love, purity, chastity, and so on, and what in the Druidic tradition we call the virtues and attributes of the same or similar species of flowers. In many cultures flowers represent various feelings and attitudes, whereas in Druidic flower magic the flower is actually made up of these virtues and attributes. Put simply, whereas in other cultures the rose represents love, in Druidic flower lore, the rose, in any of its many forms, *contains* the virtue of love, with all its wonderful qualities, and by magical workings and ritual we may transfer this esoteric asset to a particular person, imbuing him or her with the same spiritual energies as the original flower. Although we may identify other differences, such as the various species available in each culture and the ways and means by which they are used, this concept of containment is the key difference between Druidic flower magic and the use of flowers in other magic traditions.

In Druidic flower magic, an individual living flower may be given to a recipient with a dual intention. In the first intention, giving, for example, a single red rose to a recipient who is aware of the flower's virtue of inspiring and attracting love may well ignite the exact same emotion in the recipient. In this case, the shared meaning of the flower is conveyed in the same way as the meanings of flowers are expressed and conveyed through the Victorian language of flowers. The second intention is that by merely handling the flower, the recipient will absorb its virtues in a manner similar to osmosis, through the semiporous membrane of the skin. This, of course, is a much less potent technique for influencing the recipient than the flower potions we will discover in chapter 6. In the Druidic tradition, a bouquet of flowers is assembled with the intention of combining the spiritual energies they contain to achieve a specific outcome, much like individual medicinal compounds are mixed together to create an effective remedy. This Druidic bouquet differs from the Victorian tussie-mussie, which relies only on symbolic meanings, not intrinsic qualities.

DRUIDIC FLOWER MAGIC, HOMEOPATHY, AND BACH FLOWER REMEDIES

Flowers also play a part in many modern, New Age belief systems in both Eastern and Western cultures. While some of these practices may be seen in both ancient and modern Western alchemy, we see very little inclusion of it in modern-day scientific medicine. This may be mainly attributed to the fact that mainstream medicine completely rejects any nonscientific remedies and instead relies entirely upon physical chemistry and surgical interventions for its results.

The first modern influences of Druidic flower magic that we can identify are in the muddied history of what we now call alternative healing, a range of practices that have attracted more than their share of criticism and ridicule brought on mainly by accusations of quackery and amateur malpractice. One of the most familiar and widespread of these alternative practices that has its foundations in ancient flower magic is homeopathy, though, as we shall see, in many ways this practice has deliberately ignored or overlooked the most important doctrine of Druidic flower magic in favor of a pseudoscientific set of theories, and in so doing has thrown the baby out with the bathwater.

The general public was first made aware of homeopathy in 1796, following its development by German physician Samuel Hahnemann (1755–1843) as a form of alternative medicine. Hahnemann based his medical theory on the ancient Greek proposition of *similia similibus curentur,* "like cures like," suggesting that a substance that causes discernible symptoms in a healthy person is capable of curing the same symptoms when they appear in a sick person. This same doctrine was indeed a popular belief with alchemists and mediciners during the medieval era and was by no means the brainchild of Hahnemann. However many of the substances involved, particularly those derived from the plant kingdom, are poisonous if taken in even small quantities, so Hahnemann contrived to dilute them by a simple process he called homeopathic dilution, where he repeatedly diluted the original substance to the point where the eventual "remedy" contained no active ingredients or residual chemicals from its original component. Modern analysis informs us that the resultant remedies typically do not even contain a single molecule of the original material, making them biochemically inert. An indispensable aspect of the homeopathic dilution is that between each dilution—and there are many—the substance is vigorously hit and shaken, the reason being that this process apparently makes the dilution "remember" the benefits and potency of the original substance, so that when taken orally it may cure the illness or disease. Hahnemann believed that disease was caused by what he termed *miasms,* which created an imbalance in the patient's vital force, and that his remedies corrected this imbalance by countering the harmful miasms.

Think what you will of Hahnemann—and a great many people enthusiastically subscribe to the principles of homeopathy and his remedies—I mention homeopathy here simply to compare its principles to those underpinning Druidic flower magic. Just as homeopathy does not seek the direct effects of a chemical substance to produce its results and depends, instead, upon an alternative force to create a rebalance of the body's vital force, Druidic flower magic does not depend upon the chemical constituents of the flowers it employs. It instead rallies the flower's unseen, intangible, and often elusive magical properties to produce its outcomes.

Much has been written about Hahnemann and his homeopathy, and I refer the reader to the many publications and resources available rather than spend more time on the subject here, but it is worth pursuing the ideas of one of Hahnemann's later followers who focused his interest directly on the properties of the flower kingdom in a particularly purposeful way.

At the beginning of the twentieth century, a relatively unknown British doctor, homeopath, and author named Edward Bach (1886–1936), an ardent follower of Samuel Hahnemann's principles, began to develop his own theory of healing, which governed the development of what was to become the Bach flower remedies. He believed that poor health and disease resulted from an imbalance between what he called "the purpose of the soul and the personality's actions," which resulted in "energy blocking and a lack of bodily harmony, manifesting itself in a range of physical disorders."

In 1930, at the age of forty-three, Bach turned his back on his formal mainstream medical training and directed his attention to finding a new healing concept of his own. Born of Welsh parents, Bach returned to Wales to seek inspiration. He abandoned his scientific training in favor of what he described as an intuitive technique, based on his apparent psychic connection to the plants he came into contact with. He believed that his strongest intuitive connection was with flowers, and he would hold his hand over individual flowers to connect to their "emotion" and would assign the flower healing properties associated to that particular emotion. He spent the majority of the year experimenting and developing his first flower remedies. None of these contained any material part of the flower but had what Bach claimed to be the flower's "pattern of energy," absorbed in a solution that contained the vibrational nature of the flower, which defined the flower's remedial properties. These "vibrational medicines," dependent as they are on what is called "water memory," the water's ability to retain a memory of the flower's energies, must not be confused with traditional homeopathic remedies, even though they are also based on extreme dilutions in water, as they do not subscribe to many other homeopathic principles such as the Law of Similarities; however it cannot be denied that his inspiration was firmly seated in his own homeopathic learning.

Bach believed that the properties of the individual plant were absorbed in the dew. Bach observed sunlight passing through the dew that collected on flower petals each morning and determined that in this way the dew absorbed the plant's properties. He consequently began collecting this sunstruck morning dew as the first step in his new process. But he soon found that collecting dew from the various flowers he was experimenting with was laborious, and unsurprisingly, he failed to collect sufficient dew to fulfill his needs. His answer to this was to pick the various flowers and suspend them in glass vessels containing spring water so that the sun's rays could pass through them, which, in his mind, replicated the dew forming on the petals under the morning sunlight and energized the spring water in the same way. He further suggested that if this process could not be carried out, for example in the dark of the British winter when sunlight was scarce, then the flowers could simply be boiled in the spring water to obtain the same result. Whichever way it was obtained, the next step in Bach's process was to dilute the energized spring water with equal amounts of brandy to create what he termed the "mother tincture," the basis for all of his remedies. This mother tincture was then further diluted with water before it was drunk.

Bach continued to develop his process and add more plant species to his collection of flower remedies for the remainder of his life. Despite his formal scientific medical training, he was happy to justify his flower remedy theory on the basis that it incorporated the Aristotelian principle of the four elements: Earth nurtures the original plant, the air feeds it as it grows, the plant absorbs energy from the sun (which represents the Aristotelian fire), and water absorbs the flower's energies and conveys it to the user—while all of these elements combine to create the flower's healing properties.

Since his early days as a medical practitioner, Bach had been a devoted Freemason and progressed through the various degrees to become a prominent mason by the time of his death. It has been suggested that his theories may have evolved from his Freemason connections together with the elemental beliefs of the ancient alchemists, knowledge he would have encountered during his medical and homeopathy training, but as we progress through the following chapters, we will see that in many ways his theories run parallel to the Welsh Druidic lore he would have come across during his early days in North Wales, though it must be said that there are a number of fundamental differences between the Druidic flower magic we are exploring and Bach's processes, though many of these contradictions may have been ignored by Bach as a matter of convenience.

THREE

Basic Precepts of Druidic Flower Magic

Both Hahnemann and Bach developed systems that may be broadly compared with Druidic flower magic, as did the ancient Egyptians, Greeks, and Romans. Many readers may well have encountered the use of flowers in a wide range of occult disciplines, both ancient practices and recent New Age ones. It is reasonable to ask how Druidic flower magic differs from other traditions in theory, practice, and the anticipated results.

THE LIVING FORCE

In understanding Druidic flower magic, it's necessary first to understand the basic principles underlying Druidic lore. The first principle is that we do not work *with* the forces of nature; we work *within* them. Nature itself is made up of a collection of living forces and physical matter, and as we are a part of nature, we also are composed of living energies and physical matter, like all other living things. In accepting this basic philosophy, we acknowledge that in sharing these basic features, we are ourselves one of the component parts of nature and can influence and change all aspects of nature by our intentions and actions.

The second principle, of equal importance, is the belief that nature, and therefore humankind, is not controlled by any deities, internal or external, but instead exists in a constant state of chaotic flux, randomly changing without any universal objective or any universal laws. It follows therefore that as there is no god or gods responsible for the creation or the rule of the universe, much of our destiny is in our own hands, so we cannot relinquish responsibility for our endeavors, and if we fail, there is no one to blame but ourselves.

FLOWER ATTRIBUTES AND VIRTUES

Within this Druidic cosmos we find the botanical realm and a wide variety of flowering plants and, of course, the flower itself. Each plant is therefore composed of spiritual and material elements, as are all living things. Its spiritual components are made up of a portion of a universal or communal energy that it receives at its moment of fertilization, an energy that will be returned to the all-encompassing universal energy when it dies. Is also has an individual energy that it acquires at the moment of fertilization, which ceases to exist when the flower dies. Within each flower, we see that the universal or communal energy connects it to what may be call the world spirit, *spiritus mundi* or *Weltgeist,* while its individual personal energy defines it as an individual living entity. For example, an individual daisy is distinguished from all other daisies, but it is also part of the daisy species, which is distinguished from all other flower species; all flowers are also imbued with the same world spirit that animates all beings. The material component of the flower consists of the physical manifestation or visible, material presence of the flower, which decays as the flower decomposes.

Possibly the most significant difference in the Druidic tradition of flower magic is that we do not depend upon any of the physical attributes of the flowering plant we utilize, unlike many of the other ancient disciplines where flowers and other parts of flowering plants were used for their medicinal or therapeutic healing properties. The Druidic tradition uses only the magical, spiritual energies of the flowers, leaves, and occasionally the berries of the plants and does not use this form of flower magic as a healing practice.

Because Druidic flower magic uses the flower's virtues and attributes solely as a supranatural energy, it therefore assigns distinctive and atypical attributes to the range of indigenous flowering plants it employs. But even within the broader Druidic tradition, the attributes and virtues assigned to the flower may differ from those assigned to the overall plant: the flower, compared to the whole plant or other specific parts of the plant, such as roots and herbal leaves, is used in a completely different way to achieve a completely different outcome. This means that some flowers and flowering plants may appear to have different and sometimes conflicting attributes attributed to them depending upon which Druidic discipline they are being used within.

Differences in the attributes assigned to individual flowers and the way they are used in practice may also be seen between the ancient, pre-Celtic tradition, as applied here in this book, and the changes that occurred to this tradition following the arrival of the Celtic influence. The introduction of the western Gaels' previously unknown spiritual beliefs and ritual practices impacted almost every aspect of the indigenous people's culture and everyday life. Among the far-reaching changes was the introduction of flowers and flowering plants native to the European continent that had not previously grown in Britain. Thankfully, due to the uninterrupted oral tradition of the Druidic lore, these modifications are identifiable and have been eliminated from my investigation, which focuses only on the ancient, pre-Celtic tradition, its materials, processes, and intentions.

Readers may also recognize that most of the flowers used in this tradition are assigned different virtues and magical properties in other newer traditions and beliefs. This is significant in as much as the attributes listed here for a particular flower may, in some cases, contradict the use of the same flower in rituals and workings already in use. Here I must suggest that simply because I am defining the various flowers used in the Druidic lore that I have been raised in, I am in no way suggesting that it is superior or holds precedence over any other tradition or belief system. My intention is simply to help readers to explore and experiment with the beliefs that I know, understand them with an open mind, and embrace only what appeals and makes sense to their own judgments.

THE CARDINAL ESSENCES AND CRAFTING OF POTIONS

The flower has three components: petals, flower head, and leaves. Each of these three components holds within it one of the three cardinal essences of the flower. In the majority of flowers, the petals contain its universal energy, strengthened and invigorated by their association with the sun; the flower head contains the reproductive parts of the flower, which holds the flower's individual energy, ensuring that it is able to pass its unique properties on to the next generation; and the flower's leaves hold its material energy, as they are the whole plant's "engine room," converting sunlight and nutrients into material growth. But each component—petals, flower head, leaves—also contains in natural proportion the potency of the universal energy, its unique individual energy, and the material energy, combined in a single complex existence.

As with other traditions, the Druidic craft captures the flower's spiritual energies in a variety of carrier mediums, but uniquely it achieves this by separating the plant's three cardinal essences, infusing each in a separate carrier medium, elevating each to maximize its potential, and eventually reuniting all three to create the potion or elixir that is used in the magical working. Once each of these individual cardinals has been elevated, they are reunited immediately before the resulting potion is to be used. In this way, the natural balance of the plant has been maintained, and its magic balance remains intact. This primary principle is repeated time and time again, demonstrating its effectiveness in crafting potent magic devices.

For those who may have researched other Druidic-based texts, including my own, the way flowers are selected, harvested, and elevated in flower magic differs from the way they may be used in other workings even within the same tradition. In particular, those who may have read previous texts on the separation of plant cardinals will note that flower magic exclusively uses the individual flower, no matter how small it may be, as it is concerned with the magical energies of the cardinals, which are present in equal potency in both small or large flowers. The result is that the cardinal essences are crafted in much smaller volumes, and the final, reunited potion may only consist of a few drops of liquid, powder, or other carrier, whereas in other traditions, or even in other areas of practice in this tradition, larger volumes of flowers and plants are used to obtain the required results. The delicate and intricate workings of flower magic surprisingly yields equally potent potions as others using much larger quantities of botanicals and has a much greater impact on sustainability and the maintenance of renewable resources. Flower magic is therefore most appropriate for use in very specific and precisely identified needs and intended outcomes. It lends itself to being used in focused workings, and crafting the potions themselves requires precise and focused attention as very often the crafter will be working with small and fragile components.

What determines the potency of the final potion is maintaining the natural balance of the flowering plant both in the selection of which parts of the plant are used and the amount of each part used in extracting its cardinal essences. Because of the delicate balance among these three energies, we can see that if we are to maintain the flower's natural balance and vitality within our potion, then it is imperative that each is used in the same proportion as it appears in its natural state. For example, the dog rose flower has five petals, and each plant stalk has clusters of five leaves growing upon it. To extract its cardinals, we separate the five petals from the flower head to concentrate one cardinal, use the remaining flower head and its reproductive elements to concentrate the second cardinal, and all five leaves from one cluster to craft the final cardinal essence.

It is imperative then that we separate each of these cardinal essences so that we may elevate them as individual components before we reunite them to create the final potion. This separation may be done by harvesting each of the individual components without damaging or killing the plant by leaving the stem, roots, other leaves, and flower heads of the main plant untouched. It is crucial that the vitality of the plant is maintained. Within the Welsh Druidic tradition that we are exploring, crafting potions and using botanicals in other ways, such as wand crafting, creating salves, and so on, involves and depends on the botanical's vital energies.

PROVENANCE AND HARVESTING

There are two imperatives for ensuring a botanical's vital energies before we include it in any working. First, it is essential that we know the provenance of the plant we are using, which includes the location where it grew, its *terroir* (soil and climate), and what plants grew near it. These factors all influence its attributes, as do its age, how it is harvested, and how it is handled between its harvesting and use.

The second imperative is that the flower, leaves, and other parts of the plant must be used while its vital energies are still vibrant and potent. The energies contained within these essences are living, vital forces that change significantly, not only with the different stages of that plant as it matures and grows, but also within the different elements of the plant, such as the flowers, leaves, roots, and so on. As soon as any botanical is deprived of its ability to maintain its life force, such as when it is pulled up by its roots or savagely cropped or even when a plant has finished its natural life cycle, its vital energies begin to slowly dissipate, much of it returning to a communal world spirit, while its physical matter decays and nurtures later generations of plants in the same way it was nurtured by previous generations. This is a natural occurrence and cannot be avoided. The decaying process begins when we harvest the parts of the plant we intend to use, so it is imperative that we use these parts soon after they have been separated from the main plant as there is no use crafting potions with lifeless, decaying plant materials. The harvesting itself also needs to be done in the correct manner and at the correct time, which will be covered in chapter 4.

The main indicators of a botanical's freshness and suitability for use are its color, texture, and sap retention. It must have the same colors as they appear in the living plant; each leaf, petal, and flower head must retain its original living color. All the components of the flower and leaves must feel crisp and fresh to the touch, a further sign that they are still living. Finally, each component part must still retain its life-giving sap. With experience, all these criteria may be identified with confidence, and some practitioners develop an intuitive ability to recognize how much of a plant's vital energies may have been lost or are retained. Much of the vitality of these energies are contained within the sap found in all the components of the plant; as this sap evaporates or leaches from the plant, these energies dissipate as the plant dies, dries, and becomes nothing more than the physical matter, containing none of the spiritual energies of the plant but only its physical properties, which, of course, may be used for medicinal or herbal applications that do not rely on any spiritual elements for their effectiveness.

With these fundamental principles in mind, we can easily see that, within the Druidic lore, it is impossible to use store-bought materials, as we cannot know their provenance. Even if we buy from a local farm shop or grower we know, we still cannot be sure of the other aspects of the plant's provenance, such as when and how it was harvested, what other botanicals surrounded it and may have influenced its virtues, and how it has been handled since its harvest. Even if we could be assured that all these criteria were known and are acceptable, it is almost certain that the plant's vital sap and its energies will have been dispelled before it may be purchased, and all that you will be buying is its physical, material presence. This is particularly pertinent when working with flowers, as they are both the most fragile part of any plant and the most vulnerable to decay, but it is also worth bearing these facts in mind when thinking of buying any and all types of botanicals. Dried herbs may be useful for herbal remedies but they are totally ineffective in any form of Druidic magic.

Another area of practice here that is particularly important and unique in Druidic lore is the use of living wands made for a specific working while the sap is still vibrant and then the return of the wands to nature once they have been used. In Druidic lore, elaborately carved and turned wands made from seasoned wood are simply sticks.

In part 2, we shall look in great detail at how we select the appropriate flowers, gather them, and craft them into the potent potions we use in our magic.

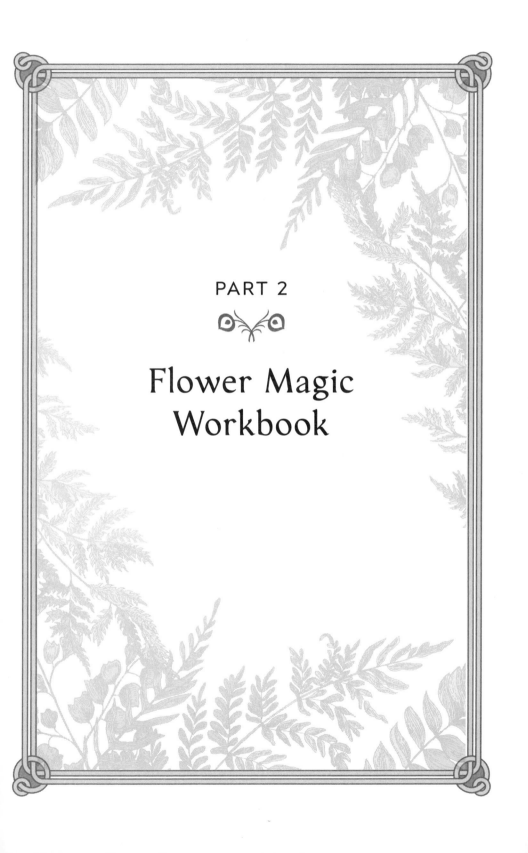

PART 2

Flower Magic
Workbook

FOUR

Identification, Selection, and Harvesting

As a means of reproduction, the flowering plant surpasses all other methods of plant reproductive distribution. The number of flowering plant species is vast and diverse, found in every country and on every continent, even Antarctica. However, as we are exploring a specific tradition, that of the lore of Welsh Druids, we can confine the range of flowering plants we use to those indigenous to the homelands of this specific belief system, those flowering plants of the British Isles, including Ireland, and much of Europe.

As noted in the introduction, many of these same plants can also be found in North America and elsewhere in the world, including Asia. If, however, the practitioner is living in a region where most of these plants cannot be found and that has a different palette of indigenous flowering plants, the same processes and methods may be used, as the principles involved are universal if combined with the overall concept of Druidic lore. Many readers may also be acutely aware of the folklore and beliefs of their region and, as such, the attributes and virtues of the flowering plants that surround them. This being the case, other indigenous flowering plants may be substituted for the plants explored in this book, but only if the practitioner is confident in the compatibility of their use and application in every case.

As an alternative to substituting flowers with similar attributes, the reader may choose to grow a selection of the plants used in this publication, reproducing the conditions necessary for them to thrive and controlling their integrity and provenance by careful supervision of their environment. To assist in this endeavor, I have included in chapter 9 instructions and guidance for creating a physic or medicinal garden specifically designed to grow many of the plants listed in the directory in chapter 10.

IDENTIFICATION

One of the things that has come to the fore in the current surge of interest in foraging wild foods is the importance of correctly identifying the plants being harvested. Though many flowering plants have similar-looking alternatives, these lookalike plants in the same family may, nonetheless, have very different characteristics, and mistakes in identification can result in skin irritations, allergies, poisoning, illness, or even death. When working with the spiritual elements of flowering plants, these differences may be even less visible to the untrained eye or undeveloped intuition, resulting in profound errors in identifying the virtues and attributes of individual flowers and negating their influences in any workings in which they are included. So correctly identifying the flowering plants we use in spiritual and magic workings is just as imperative as it is with edible plants, and, unfortunately, the results can be equally as devastating.

Another aspect that adds to the confusion of correctly identifying flowering plants is that most plants are identified by different names in different traditions. Most people will know the plants in their locality by one or more folklore names as well as a more comprehensive common name. These folk names may refer to the plant's shape, color, or traditional use, and many of us first become aware of these folk names as children, long before we get to know their more widespread names. In the tradition of the Welsh Druids, many of these local names are based in the Welsh language, both Old Welsh and in the modern usage, which adds another level of confusion. Similarly, these Welsh names vary significantly within the principality, where distinct differences appear in the use and pronunciation of the language between the north, south, east, and west versions of what was originally a tribal language. Unfortunately, we can find no overall conformity even in the scientific naming of some of these plants as, again, the confusion between the modern and ancient names, the Greek, Latin, and occasional Arabic names, and other inconsistencies may fail to make identification easy. If we turn to the medieval manuscripts and herbaria, we find even greater confusion with a muddle of classical languages, folk names, common names, misspellings, and even names created by the scribes, who appeared to have no compunction about changing the original texts into something they found more interesting.

Identifying Edible and Poisonous Flowers

A good number of the indigenous flowers used here are edible, but it should be said that although some are believed to be beneficial in their own right, others may be classed as edible but benign. Once again it is important to emphasize the importance of correct identification of any plant classed as edible and to be aware that in some cases only certain parts of the plant may be edible while other parts may indeed be harmful. The flower directory in chapter 10 specifies which of the flowering plants listed are edible, but please be aware that no provision is made for any form of allergies that may be present in the consumer. Again, there is no safe substitute for diligent research and learning and correct application.

Having considered the range of potentially edible flowering plants, it is equally important to consider those flowering plants listed as poisonous. If the practitioner has even the slightest notion that a flowering plant or any separate part of a flowering plant is poisonous, then it must be avoided at all costs. Here it is once again important to be aware that individuals may be allergic to specific plants that in general may not be considered poisonous. Avoid using any flowering plant that may be harmful either when applied topically or ingested.

The message contained within this warning is to take great care in selecting the flowering plant and only use plants that you can identify with confidence. Use an illustrated plant guide or field guide and carefully read any information about the characteristics of the plant you are seeking to identify.

Never use a plant that you do not know or are unsure whether you have identified correctly.

Flowering Trees, Thorns, and Berries

In addition to what many people would consider flowers, produced by ground-living flowering plants, it is also important to recognize the significance of trees that produce flowers as part of their life cycle, as these have a particular place in Druidic flower magic. The indigenous flowering trees that are most common in this tradition are listed in detail in the flower directory in chapter 10, and potions using their flowers are crafted in exactly the same way as with ground-flowering plants.

Many readers will be familiar with the blossoming of beautifully delicate flowers on thorn bushes and briars prior to the appearance of their berries in the autumn. These prolific flowers are used in very specific ways in Druidic flower magic, and we will focus intently upon this in a later section, where we will see that the potency of these unique flowers is enhanced by incorporating a wand crafted from the same plant in their crafting and casting. In other instances, the delicate flowers of the blackberry, raspberry, and others are used in the same way as other ground-flowering plants.

SELECTING THE FLOWERS TO BE USED

The selection of exactly which flower is most appropriate for each individual circumstance depends entirely upon conforming to six codependent core principles.

1. Each flower type is invested with one or more natural attributes and virtues that may be used to the advantage of the practitioner or their subject without damaging the host plant.

2. These specific attributes and virtues are held within the flowering plant as three distinct spiritual cardinal essences, each vested in a separate component part of the plant as we explored in chapter 3.

3. Each of these cardinal essences may be extracted from the flowering plant by various means (described in chapter 5), still retaining their natural attributes and potency.

4. Each of these separate cardinal essences may have its virtues and attributes elevated by an arcane Druidic spiritual working that both cleanses it and amplifies its potency.

5. When these three individual cardinal essences are reunited, they produce a powerful potion or elixir that contains the elevated spiritual virtues and attributes of the original flower.

6. This potent elixir may be used to cast and bind a beneficial intention to a targeted subject, place, artifact, or atmosphere. (Note that *intention* is the Druidic word for *spell* and is used hereafter for the potion recipes in chapter 6.)

From these six principles, we can see that the selection of the flowering plant that holds the most appropriate cardinals is paramount to the success of the eventual intention. In other words, if we begin with the wrong flower(s), then we have no chance of obtaining the beneficial result we are seeking. So how exactly do we decide which flowering plant is the most appropriate donor plant for our specific need?

Generation after generation of Druids, stretching back to the beginning of the emerging population of the British Isles, developed a unique relationship with and understanding of the natural world that surrounded them. One small part of that understanding was the discovery that each individual flowering plant contains beneficial attributes, both in the physical, material world and within the spiritual strata of our existence. Physically, many have medicinal and general health benefits that are readily identified by the modern-day scientific and pharmaceutical community. Spiritually, mainstream culture has been slow in acknowledging the spiritual benefits that these plants provide. Having said that, recent advances in alternative and complementary medicine celebrate a wide range of benefits emerging from many of the flowering plants belonging to the ancient principles of Druidic flower magic, though it must be said that many more have been overlooked and remain to be discovered.

Within this arcane Druidic lore, we still retain the knowledge of which flowering plant contains which attribute and virtue. In broad terms, these may be seen in each individual flower listed in the flower directory in chapter 10; however, this notional separation of individual attributes and virtues and their association with individual flowering plants and their component parts is only apparent when the plant grows in isolation, without the influences of the terroir in which it grows or the other plants that may surround it. It also suggests that every specific flower and plant within a particular species retains all its attributes and virtues no matter how or when it is harvested. However, we know that this is never the case: no plant grows in isolation, and if a flower is harvested randomly, then we cannot guarantee that it has retained all or any of its benefits.

We see then that the first step in selecting a donor plant is to determine which species holds the attributes and virtues we are seeking, and for this we can refer to the flower directory in chapter 10 with proven confidence. Once we know which flower species we wish to use, we must find it growing in its natural environment. The alternative of growing the plant in a physic or medicinal garden is explored in chapter 9, so we will ignore that option at this point.

Searching the natural environment for a specific wild plant can be a daunting task and is hugely dependent upon where the practitioner lives. For me, living in the far west of Ireland, this often means a brief stroll along the pathways and woodland that surround my home, but for someone living in a densely populated urban setting, this may involve a lengthy and difficult road trip to a more productive location. Unfortunately, for urban dwellers, there may not be a simple alternative, as store-bought botanicals, whether sold fresh or dried, are not an acceptable alternative as their provenance cannot be defined. If possible, within the space constraints of the individual, the recommended alternative would be the type of physic garden outlined in chapter 9.

Having already defined the importance of being able to identify the desired plant correctly and the consequences of harvesting the wrong botanical, we must now consider the impact of the plant's location. As noted earlier, terroir refers to the environment and climate in which a plant is growing and is often used in the world of wine making to describe the environmental factors that influence a wine's character. Similar environmental considerations also drive the tea and coffee industries. All of the producers involved in these industries readily acknowledge that variations in growing conditions have a profound influence on the strength and complexity of flavor of their produce, and in the same way, the terroir in which a flowering plant grows acutely influences its suitability and potency when used in the crafting of flower magic potions and elixirs.

Specifically, the climate in the sense of temperature, rainfall, frost, and so on of any particular year or season has profound consequences on the blooming period of all flowering plants. In the same way, the location of a flowering plant, whether beneath a canopy within a forest or in the shadow of a larger plant, will also influence the development of the plant and its flowers. Other circumstances that influence the potency and life cycle of the plant include soil composition, groundwater supply, the presence of plant predators (animals, insects, fungi), and air and water pollution, along with any other physical factors that may affect the physical development of the plant.

When considering the external spiritual influences on the desired plant, another significant factor to take into account is what plants are growing near it. No plant grows in isolation and most grow in close proximity to other plants, such as ivy, fungi, trees, mosses, or other species of plants, often with their roots or foliage intertwined. Some, like the mistletoe, so frequently associated with the Druidic tradition, grow as parasitic partners, depending upon the nutrients of their host plant for their survival. While these neighboring plants have an obvious physical impact on the targeted plant, they also have an even more profound influence on their spiritual characteristics. This influence may be predictable, or in some cases it may be unforeseeable.

Where the surrounding botanicals are identifiable, it is not difficult to interpret the influence they may have upon the targeted plant and whether its effects will be beneficial or harmful. This aspect of the influence one plant may have upon its neighbor is used to advantage in physic gardens where selected plants are planted together as companion plants to the benefit of both. In the wild, the distribution of botanicals is far more random, so particular attention must be paid to the plants growing in close proximity to the targeted one and due consideration given to the influences they may have on the plant intended to be harvested.

HARVESTING

There are typically very few occasions when a plant is harvested without careful planning beforehand. To do this we need to look in detail at the Druidic tenets that inform the harvesting process.

One of the core principles that underpin Druidic lore is a fundamental respect for the balance of nature or what we now call conservation or environmental responsibility, which means harvesting in a sensitive and sustainable way. This principle applies not only to harvesting botanicals but also to any earth-given resource, including minerals, animals, aquatic life, water, and other vulnerable resources. In simplified terms, this means not taking any threatened species or depleting small communities of plants and having a responsible approach to taking and using any natural resource, which in practice means, for example, only harvesting the parts of botanicals that are needed while leaving roots intact when possible, not damaging the bark of trees, and, in general, not compromising the health of any living plants or animals in your work. In addition, all used or surplus materials are returned to their original source when your work is complete.

Assuming these basic tenets will be respected, other considerations in planning plant harvesting include the seasonal cycle, the time of harvesting (day or night), the weather at the time of harvesting, and how much time will pass until the harvested plant is processed. Each of these variables has an impact on the spiritual energies of the plant, so we need to look at each in detail.

Seasonal Cycle

One of the other major considerations to be taken into account is the season in which the plant and/or flowers are harvested. This is not to be confused with the life cycle of the botanical involved but is of course determined by the blossoming period of the flowering plant; depending upon the species, the flowers will appear at specific times of the year, be it spring, summer, autumn, or, in a few instances, winter.

For many plants, the appearance of their flowers is an essential part of their life cycle and reproductive process. Some produce flowers once a year, others twice a year, yet others once every two years, and some flower once in periods of anything up to twenty years. If we are to utilize the virtues and attributes of any particular flower, then it is essential that we understand its flowering cycle so that we can predict the flowering season and plan our workings—so that we know which flowers are available at which time and plan the crafting and storage of specific potions so that they are available at the time when they may be needed. The flowering periods of all the plants referred to in this book are listed in the flower directory, which appears in chapter 10. These flowering periods are for Northwestern Europe, specifically the British Isles, and will differ for other parts of the world. Please consult a field guide for flowering times in your area and also for other flowering plants not listed in the directory.

Here, though, we are discussing the season in which the flower is harvested, not when it first appears. As with the other aspects of harvesting, the date must be meticulously planned. In practice, flowers and plants harvested in the spring will be highly energized, with abundant vitality. Those harvested in the summer months will have a high potency and are at the peak of their ability to influence success. Plants harvested in the autumn are at their most mature, with a deep, lasting influence and are ideal for binding workings. Finally, plants harvested during the winter period have the characteristics of longevity and perseverance and are best suited to health and wisdom workings.

In relation to how these characteristics may be best utilized, they may be summarized as follows:

Spring-harvested plants: Impart maximum vitality and energy, ideal for workings relating to new relationships or desired relationships, regenerating relationships and affection, revitalizing sexual relationships or rekindling relationships in general. They are also particularly useful in divination, as the piercing energy of the plant accesses energies buried deep within time and memory.

Summer-harvested plants: Have the potency and vigor to be used in the most difficult and challenging workings. They are considered to be the most powerful of plants, harvested at the zenith of their potency. Ideally suited to workings intent on achieving a successful outcome for a task or activity, fulfilling desires and banishing failure.

Autumn-harvested plants: Have the ability to influence deeply, intensely, and with long lasting effect. Best suited to binding workings, outcomes expected to last over time, and problem solving in general.

Winter-harvested plants: Are ideal for workings related to good health, perseverance, and long life. These plants are also suitable in workings seeking wisdom, clarity of mind, and practical outcomes.

Time of Day at Harvesting

The next consideration to take into account when planning your harvesting is the time of day at which you intend to harvest. All botanicals are influenced by the progress of the daylight to night time, some more than others. Some are classified as heliotropic, which means they slowly change their orientation, following the progress of the sun through the daytime sky. Others, like the daisy, only open their flowers once the sun has risen and close their flower heads when the sun sets. Hence their original name, "day's eyes," meaning they only open their "eyes" or flowers during daylight. In many older languages, like old Welsh and old English, these more descriptive names still remain. It is important therefore to be aware of the influence of the sun (daytime harvesting) and the moon (nighttime harvesting) on the virtues of the flowers you intend to use.

In general terms, those flowers harvested in daylight are strong and vibrant in their effect and best used for potions intended for men, while those harvested under moonlight are more subtle in their influences, slower working but longer lasting and best suited for potions intended to influence females. Your harvesting times should be planned accordingly.

Weather at Time of Harvesting

Whether the flowers you choose to use are harvested during the day or night, the prevailing weather conditions will have a distinct impact upon their virtues and influences. When flowers are gathered in fine weather, their virtues are clearly defined by the other aspects considered above. If they are harvested in the rain, their virtues are diluted but purified in their simplest form. Importantly, if flowers are harvested during a thunder storm their influences are particularly powerful, amplified by the power of the thunder; if they are gathered during a period of lightning, then they are considered to be at their most potent, with the most powerful effect. While it may be difficult and sometimes dangerous to plan your harvesting during a thunder or lightning storm, if this is possible, the resultant elixirs or potions are considered to be extra potent and powerful and are used accordingly.

Timing of Harvesting and Crafting

No matter how or when you harvest your selected flower, if it is not handled correctly directly following the harvesting, it is very likely that its virtues and influences will be at best considerably diluted or distorted, or even destroyed or nullified. It is important to remember that *all* the flowers used to craft potions must be correctly harvested and used as soon as possible after they are collected. Any delay in using the harvested flowers may negatively affect their influence and virtues. As a result, we must therefore also take into account exactly when the flower is to be crafted into a potion when planning the harvesting. Needless to say, it is not possible to dry or otherwise preserve and store the flowers until they are needed. During the period between harvesting and crafting, the flower should be safely stored in a dark, cool place, away from any external influences, thereby retaining all the positive aspects that the practitioner has worked so hard to preserve.

In this chapter, we have considered the importance of knowing the true provenance of every resource we use. Having now considered the methods of correctly targeting the desired plant, the external influences that may affect it, and the various aspects of harvesting that may change its virtues, it is clear that knowing the origin and means of the harvesting of any plant is imperative and that no store-bought plants or flowers can be used for our purpose.

With the intended flower correctly harvested and stored, the next step in producing our potion is to look in detail at the crafting process itself—the principles involved and the specifics of crafting the various types of potions that we may require.

FIVE

Methods for Extracting the Three Cardinal Essences

While we understand that the ancient Druids would have had little, if any, of what we would now call scientific knowledge, their legacy shows us that they had a profound awareness of the natural world and how many of its products, both spiritual and material, could be used to benefit the communities they served, in particular the vast range of botanicals that grow wild in the British Isles. In accessing this secret realm of flower magic, it is not necessary to become a botany graduate, or even to have formal scientific training; all that is required is to understand the world of flowering plants in the same way as our Druidic ancestors. This understanding enabled them to conjure magic intentions and craft magic potions for every purpose and need.

In chapter 4, we investigated how we identify the flowering plants to be used for each specific purpose along with explaining just how each should be harvested and handled until it is used. Here we will concentrate on how the magical cardinal essences of the individual components of the flowering plant are extracted so that they may be elevated before being reunited to create the final potion. But first we must describe how we identify the individual component parts of the flowering plant that we intend to use.

Flowering plants grow in myriad forms and shapes, some with single flower heads, some with multiple flower heads, and others with flowers that are so diverse that it may be difficult to even identify them as flowers. No single publication of this kind can hope to include details of every available flowering plant and how to utilize its magical essences. As this publication is concerned exclusively with Druidic flower magic, I have therefore confined the variety of flowering plants to those of the homelands of the Druids as we know them, giving preference to those used most frequently by our Druidic ancestors. However, as noted in the introduction, many of these plants are not exclusive to the British Isles and can be found throughout Europe and North America and also Eurasia and North Africa.

To today's scientist, the Druidic understanding of flowering plants and their structure may seem naive and simplistic, but we know from their legacy that they were able to utilize the plants at their disposal on a material level, crafting cures, medications, and foods, and on a spiritual level in magic and spiritual workings in a wide range of circumstances. It is to these magic and spiritual workings that we shall now turn our attention.

We learned in chapter 3 that the use of flowering plants in Druidic magic required the extraction and elevation of the three cardinal essences contained within the plant being used. Each of these vital essences is concentrated in a particular part of the plant, and differing magic disciplines depend upon accessing different components of the plant for their work. In some forms of Druidic magic, we extract cardinals from roots, stems, barks, leaves, fruits, berries, and flowers, as different cardinals, used for different purposes, are found in all parts of the plant. Here, however, we are focusing our exploration on flower magic, which for the greater part utilizes the flower head, subdivided into the petals and the reproductive components, and the leaves growing on the flower stalk. We are then using the entire flower as we normally know it except for the stalk, which in this case is seen as the conduit or pipeline that carries the vital sap to the head and leaves of the flower.

Having harvested the desired flower in the correct manner, the first step in extracting the three cardinal essences is to deconstruct the flower into its component parts, by which we mean the flower head with its reproductive elements, the petals, and the leaves. If the flower has been harvested correctly, we will have exactly the same number of leaves as there are petals on the flower in order to maintain the natural balance of the flower. The petals are carefully removed from the flower head and placed aside. The flower head is detached from the stalk as close to the base of the head as possible, thereby removing all of the stalk from the head. The leaves are detached from the stalk as close to the stalk as possible, leaving the short leafstalk attached to the leaf. At this point, the remaining stalk may be discarded by returning it to its original growing place and placing it on the ground with a brief incantation of thanks. The three flower components, each containing its own individual cardinal essence, are now separated and ready for the working that extracts their individual essence or energy.

There are a number of methods for extracting the flower's cardinal essences, each one having its own advantages. They are described in order of increasing potency of the essence produced.

The separated component parts of a flower, ready for the next stage of extracting their cardinal essences. (See also color plate 3.)

1. **Maceration or Cold Infusion.** The first and most common method is extraction by maceration, allowing the flower parts to stand in contact with a solvent carrier that absorbs the cardinal essence, its virtues and attributes. In maceration, flower parts are soaked or steeped at ambient room temperature in a carrier solvent in a tightly sealed container. In this case the carrier solvent may be spring water, carrier oils (typically hazelnut or walnut), syrups (such as honey or maple), glycerin, alcohol, or even dry powders.

2. **Decoction.** The second method, one we will all be familiar with, is decoction, where the individual components of the flower are steeped in a hot or warm carrier solvent in the same way we regularly make tea, although typically this process requires a longer infusion period. Here the carrier solvent is most commonly spring water, oils, or syrups.

3. **Distillation.** The third method is that of distillation, which may be done in a variety of ways. The most common form of distillation is steam, where the individual component parts of the flower are distilled separately by placing them in a still and passing hot steam through them, extracting the essential oil from the flower parts and creating a less potent floral water as a useful by-product. This method of extraction requires the most skill, particularly as the individual component parts of a single flower are so small that the process requires a great deal of understanding and experience to achieve the desired results.

4. **Fermentation.** The fourth and final method we shall explore is extraction by fermentation, where each component part of the flower is individually fermented in a process similar to wine making or the making of beer, cider, and mead.

In deciding which method to use it is important to give clear thought to how and why the intended potion is to be used. Even at this early stage in crafting there are fundamental choices that must be made. Each of these methods, which are detailed below, produces a different form and potency of potion, some concentrated and crafted in small quantities, others less potent and produced in slightly larger volumes. Some are water based, others have oil or alcohol carriers, yet other methods produce a dry powder potion, ideally suited for particular uses. Water-based potions are best used in situations that require wider distribution of the potion, such as in laying across tracks or thresholds to bar or banish unwanted energies and intentions, or circling work spaces to provide protection. Oil-based potions are best suited for times when the virtue of the potion needs to linger for a while, particularly in the case of love philters and other attraction potions. Alcohol carrier solvents are perfect in cases where the intention needs to be quickly absorbed, such as when it is cast onto a garment for protection or when traveling or if is applied secretly to a garment to be worn by the recipient. Other carrier solvents, such as glycerin, syrup, or ointments, have their own most suitable applications, and in time the practitioner will gain the experience and develop sufficient intuition to be able to select the most appropriate carrier solution for each circumstance, bearing in mind that some of the carrier solutions may only be used in certain methods of extraction. For example, a syrup carrier may not be used in the distillation process, and likewise, a powder carrier is unsuitable for fermentation.

Note: None of these potions may be taken internally, no matter how they are extracted or what carrier is used.

We shall now look at each extraction process in turn and give detailed instructions on how to achieve the best results in every case.

MACERATION OR COLD INFUSION

In its simplest form maceration or cold infusion is the process of steeping or soaking a material, in this case the component parts of the selected flower, in a liquid or powder carrier at ambient room temperature to infuse the carrier with the attributes and virtues of the original material. The parts and the carrier are sealed in a container for six to nine days. This is the simplest form of extraction and lends itself to the largest range of carrier solvents. These include spring water, any natural carrier oil (remembering that the carrier oil itself will contain its own attributes and virtues, which may amplify or negate those of the flower being used), a range of natural syrups such as honey, maple, and so on (again, each has its own attributes and virtues), glycerin, alcohol (producing a tincture), and powders, such as chalk, dried clays, and boles.

We shall look at three different methodologies: extraction using spring water, a carrier oil (hazelnut oil), and a powder (naturally occurring chalk deposits). The method for elevating the cardinals, reuniting them, and casting the eventual potions are described in chapter 6.

Infusion Using Cold Spring Water

Equipment Needed

Maceration or cold infusion with spring water may be achieved using the simplest of equipment: three individual small sealable bottles and a vessel containing a small amount of spring water. The spring water must be from a known source of pure spring water and should be spiritually cleansed before it is used.

Most Suitable Flowers

Cold infusion using spring water is suitable for flowers of all sizes and types. The listings in the directory of flowers in the last section of this book gives information on the attributes and virtues of each.

Method

First cleanse the working stone (workbench or table) and secure it within a protective circle (see the information on the following page for instructions for preparing the work area). Assemble your equipment on your work table.

Place each of the component parts of the flower into separate small bottles or jars—the flower head into one, the petals into another, and the leaves into the last. Fill each bottle or jar with sufficient spring water to cover the flower parts.

Seal all three bottles or jars and place in a location where they will be in sunlight during the day and moonlight during the night.

The separated component parts of a flower being macerated to extract their cardinal essences. (See also color plate 4.)

Leave to macerate for a minimum of six days and a maximum of nine days.

If the individual cardinal essences are not to be reunited immediately, the separate bottles or jars may be safely stored in a cool, dark place for up to six months, with the flower parts remaining in place and the bottles or jars remaining sealed.

Preparing, Cleansing, and Protecting Your Working Stone

A working stone was originally a large recumbent stone positioned opposite the entry portal of a Druidic stone circle. This stone was and still is regularly used as the equivalent to an altar and workbench for many Druidic workings and rites. Unfortunately, many readers will not have access to such a precious resource, but this does not prevent effective workings from being undertaken by resourceful practitioners. A working stone may be substituted with a simple table or bench, preferably constructed from a natural material such as wood, bamboo, iron, or similar.

Cleansing the work space is an essential first step in all Druidic workings; the aim is to ensure that no unwelcome, malevolent energies are present that may interfere with or affect the outcome of the intended activity. This spiritual cleansing is achieved either with the use of a living wand or stave or by sprinkling moon-cleansed water on the area, working stone, or implements.

If using a living wand or stave, the wand/stave is held in the hand and a cleansing intention is spoken as the practitioner circles the area or work space. The cleansing intention, as with all intentions, should be composed by the practitioner for the specific circumstance and may be spoken aloud or recited silently. It may be as follows or similar:

> I invoke the ever-present energies of nature and ask that they eliminate from this space any unwanted, malevolent energies that may impede my planned workings. May any unwelcome energies be purged from this space and may it be purified and cleansed for the good works of nature that follow.

The working stone or table may then be placed within a simple protective circle crafted by casting a circle of sea salt around the stone, large enough to allow the practitioner to enter and move around when conducting the rite. The circle is first cast by sprinkling the sea salt on the ground to form the periphery of the circle, leaving a gap opposite the working stone as an entry portal. Before sealing the circle, the practitioner ensures all the equipment needed for the working is placed on the stone.

When all is in place, the protective circle is sealed by completing the circle with the remaining sea salt. Typically, an invocation is used to seal the circle, such as:

I now close this protective circle, sealing it and preventing the influence of any malign intents or negative energy.

Once the working stone is set up and the circle has been cast and sealed, a number of workings would typically be carried out while all is in place.

Infusion Using a Cold Carrier Oil

Equipment Needed

Cold infusion using a carrier oil, such as hazelnut oil, may also be achieved by using simple equipment: two individual small crucibles and a small sealable bottle and a vessel containing a small amount of the chosen carrier oil. The type of carrier oil may be decided by the practitioner, bearing in mind that each oil, as a natural resource, contains its own attributes and virtues that will influence the characteristics of the flower's cardinal essences either by amplifying them or by negating them; therefore careful consideration must be given to which oil is used. Whichever oil is chosen, it should be spiritually cleansed before it is used.

Most Suitable Flowers

Cold infusion with a carrier oil is best suited to small flowers or delicate flowers of all types. The directory of flowers in chapter 10 gives information on the attributes and virtues of each flower. Chapter 6 contains an example of using this method to extract the cardinal essences of a small dandelion to craft a sex magic potion.

Method

Having cleansed the working stone (workbench or table) and secured it within a protective circle, assemble your equipment on your work table (see the instructions for preparing the work area).

Place the petals of the flower into one of the small crucibles. Do the same with the flower head. Place the leaves of the flower into the small sealable bottle.

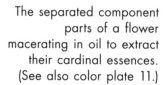

The separated component parts of a flower macerating in oil to extract their cardinal essences. (See also color plate 11.)

Fill each crucible and the jar with sufficient hazelnut oil to cover the flower parts.

Seal the bottle containing the leaves and cover the two crucibles with clear glass panes and place in a location where they will be in sunlight during the day and moonlight during the night.

Leave to macerate for a minimum of six days and a maximum of nine days.

If the individual cardinal essences are not to be reunited immediately, the separate vessels may be safely stored in a cool, dark place for up to six months, with the flower parts remaining in place and the vessels remaining sealed.

Infusion Using a Powder

Equipment Needed

Cold infusion of a powder (such as a naturally occurring chalk deposit) may be achieved by using the simplest of equipment: three individual small flat vessels, a small pane of clear glass capable of covering all three small flat vessels, and a container of the powder to be used. The type of carrier powder may be decided by the practitioner, bearing in mind that each natural powder, earth, or bole, as a natural resource, contains its own attributes and virtues that will influence the characteristics of the flower's cardinal essences, either by amplifying them or by negating them; therefore, careful consideration must be given to which powder is used. Whichever powder is chosen, it should be spiritually cleansed before it is used.

Most Suitable Flowers

Cold infusion in a powder is suitable for all flowers. The directory of flowers in chapter 10 gives information on the attributes and virtues of each flower. In chapter 6 is an example of a well-being potion crafted from ragwort cold-infused in chalk from a naturally occurring deposit.

Method

Having cleansed the working stone (workbench or table) and secured it within a protective circle, assemble your equipment on your work table (see page 50 for instructions for preparing the work area).

Fill each of the small vessels half-way with the chosen powder, leaving sufficient room for the flower parts.

The separated component parts of a flower macerating in chalk powder to extract their cardinal essences. (See also color plate 14.)

Place the petals of the flower onto the powder in one of the small vessels. Do the same with the flower head and the leaves of the flower.

Cover each of the flower parts with sufficient powder to completely immerse them.

Cover the three small flat vessels with a clear glass pane and place in a location where they will be in sunlight during the day and moonlight during the night.

Leave to macerate for a minimum of six days and a maximum of nine days.

If the individual cardinal essences are not to be reunited immediately, the separate small flat vessels may be safely stored in a cool, dark place for up to six months, with the flower parts still remaining in place and the vessels remaining covered.

The three maceration/cold infusion examples given above may be adapted to suit whichever carrier solution is to be used. The most important consideration is that the process described is only the first step in crafting the eventual potion and the individual cardinal essences must remain *separate* until they are to be used.

DECOCTION

The second method is one most people will be familiar with: extraction by decoction. In decoction the carrier liquid is infused by soaking the source material in the liquid while it is hot. Most people would have used this method in making tea or coffee. The hot carrier liquid is capable of releasing additional essential oils and other characteristics from the source material in a more efficient way than a cold carrier solvent. The two principal methods of decoction are either pouring the hot solvent liquid onto the source material and allowing it to soak or immersing the source material in the solvent liquid and heating it. In both cases, great care must be taken not to oversoak the source material as this may result in releasing unwanted elements, such as when tea is overbrewed.

In the case of the extraction of cardinal essences from flower parts, the decoction may use hot spring water, warm carrier oil, or hot syrup. It is not advisable to use alcohol in this particular process. Here we shall only look at the process of decoction using hot spring water, as essentially the same sequence of operations is used for oil and syrup.

Extraction by Decoction Using Hot Spring Water

Equipment Needed

Extraction by decoction may be achieved by using very simple equipment: three small heatproof vessels and a vessel of boiling spring water. The spring water should be spiritually cleansed before it is heated.

Most Suitable Flowers

Extraction by decoction is suitable for all flowers. The directory of flowers in chapter 10 gives information on the attributes and virtues of each flower. Chapter 6 contains an example of using this method to extract the cardinal essences of meadow buttercup to craft an attraction potion.

Method

Having cleansed the working stone (workbench or table) and secured it within a protective circle, assemble your equipment on your work table (see page 50 for instructions for preparing the work area).

Place the petals of the flower into a small heatproof vessel. Do the same with the flower head, and with the leaves of the flower.

It is important to remember that working with individual small flowers, such as the buttercup, is a delicate and precise process. Separating the individual petals, cropping the flower head, and cutting away each leaf requires focus and dexterity. For the new practitioner, this may seem a daunting task, but repeated practice and experience brings with it the skills that may at first be lacking. Similarly, the amount of water or other carrier is by necessity small and must be handled with great care. The final potion is again small, but do not underestimate its potency. Never be tempted to craft the potion using more than one flower, no matter how small it may be, as the cardinal essences must be extracted from the same *single* plant to maintain the natural balance of the reunited potion. This is essential no matter what method of extraction is being used.

Heat sufficient spring water to cover each of the flower parts in all three vessels.

Cover each of the flower parts with sufficient hot spring water to completely immerse them.

Allow the spring water to cool to room temperature then transfer each liquid and flower component to a small sealable storage bottle and seal tightly.

Place the three sealed vessels in a location where they will be in sunlight during the day and moonlight during the night.

Leave to macerate for a minimum of six days and a maximum of nine days.

If the individual cardinal essences are not to be reunited immediately, store in a cool, dark place for up to six months, with the flower parts remaining in place and the vessels remaining firmly sealed.

As noted earlier, the same method can be used for carrier oil (but only warm the oil, do not heat it to the boiling point) or syrup.

The separated component parts of a flower steeping in hot spring water solvent to extract their cardinal essences. (See also color plate 7.)

DISTILLATION

The third method of extracting the flower's cardinal essences is by distillation. This is by far the most complex and expensive technique, requiring the use of a small distillation still, specifically designed for the purpose. This method is not suited to distilling cardinal essences from small flowers because, as we shall see, the individual flower components must be of a certain size for the process to work effectively. The most suitable distillation method in this case is steam extraction distillation, similar to that used to extract essential oils. This method depends upon a quantity of a single flower component, such as flower petals, the flower head, or leaves, to be sealed in a column above a water vessel, which is than heated to produce steam. The steam flows over the flower parts and in doing so extracts its cardinal essences and captures them within the water vapor. This vapor then passes over the still to arrive at the condensing coil where it is cooled and condenses into a liquid. The resulting liquid is composed of two parts: the flower's essential oil, which floats upon the floral water, and a fragrant water infused with the perfumes and energies of the original flower part. In making essential oils, the oil floating on top of the floral water is siphoned off, but as both liquids now contain the flower part's cardinal essence, in our case we keep both liquids together. We can see then that this process is both complicated and time consuming as each flower component must be distilled separately to obtain the individual cardinals before they are reunited and used as a potion. It is also apparent that each individual flower component must be of sufficient size for the process to work effectively, bearing in mind that only one single flower can be used to produce any individual potion.

There are a number of still designs that may be used for this form of steam distillation, but here we will focus upon a single type: the split top rotating column copper alembic still.

The specific instructions for using the still are supplied with the equipment, but in principle the process is the same as is specified above. Importantly, each flower component must be distilled separately and stored in a sealed bottle or jar in a cool, dark place until all three are elevated and reunited to make the finished potion.

Plate 1. A typical split top rotating column copper alembic still used in the process of steam distillation of flower parts to extract their cardinal essences.

Plate 2. The flower of the dog rose.

Plate 3. The separated component parts of a dog rose flower, ready for the next stage of extracting their cardinal essences.

Plate 4. The separated component parts of a dog rose flower macerating in cold spring water solvent to extract their cardinal essences.

Plate 5. The flower of the meadow buttercup.

Plate 6. The separated component parts of a meadow buttercup flower, ready for the next stage of extracting their cardinal essences.

Plate 7. The petals of a meadow buttercup flower steeping in hot spring water to extract their cardinal essences.

Plate 8. The cut branch of a blood-thorn briar to be used in crafting a hook wand.

Plate 9. A single thorn from a blood-thorn briar macerating in mead.

Plate 10. The flower of the dandelion.

Plate 11. The separated component parts of a dandelion flower, macerating to extract their cardinal essences.

Plate 12. The ragwort flower.

Plate 13. The separated component parts of a ragwort flower, ready for the next stage of extracting their cardinal essences.

Plate 14. The separated component parts of a ragwort flower, lying in chalk carrier powder to extract their cardinal essences.

Plate 15. The separated component parts of a ragwort flower, completely covered in chalk carrier powder to extract their cardinal essences.

Plate 16. The completed powder potion stored in a silver box along with a feather in readiness for the casting.

Plate 17. Freshly harvested botanicals selected for the flower pouch complex along with the black velvet pouch.

Plate 18. The layout of a typical working stone, prepared for the coalescing of two cardinal essences in crafting a complex philter. The photograph shows two small bottles containing the flower potions, a small ceramic bowl for combining the potions, the practitioner's short wand (a shortened wand used in the same way as a standard wand), and a blue glass potion bottle to hold the finished complex.

A typical split top rotating column copper alembic still used in the process of steam distillation of flower parts to extract their cardinal essences. (See also color plate 1.)

It should also be noted that the same results may be obtained by using other types of stills, such as a traditional Alquitar still, a standard alembic still (much used by ancient alchemists), or an Arrastre de Vapor distilling system, all of which produce the same result, although by slightly different means. All of these distillation systems may be researched online and most are available for purchase through reputable online suppliers worldwide. Whichever way the practitioner acquires his or her distillation system, it is important to obtain the smallest capacity system available, no larger than a maximum of one liter, bearing in mind that the flower materials in the majority of cases will be very small indeed, requiring very little distillation liquid to extract their cardinal essences.

FERMENTATION

The fourth and final method of extracting the flower's cardinal essences explored here is extraction by fermentation. This process will be recognized by readers familiar with the fermentation of wines or beers, but in this case the primary fermentation material is honey and the individual flower components are fermented separately for each cardinal essence.

This method is not suited to extracting cardinal essences from small flowers because, as we shall see once again, the individual flower components must be of a certain size for the process to work effectively. This method is closely linked to the fermenting or brewing of mead and is most often used as an offshoot when the practitioner may be fermenting larger quantities of mead or *metheglyn* (an ancient form of medicinal or magic mead popular within the Welsh Druidic tradition). The process is not difficult, particularly to those who may be familiar with wine making or brewing beers, but it is time consuming as the fermentation process may take up to a month to complete. It is further complicated by the fact that both the flower components and the other materials used in the process are employed in very small quantities, and each flower component must be fermented separately, meaning that all three cardinal essences may be extracted separately by concurrent fermentation processes.

One of the misconceptions of this process is that the flower components can be simply steeped in alcohol that has been previously fermented. This is not the case. To extract the cardinals at their most potent, the flower components must be included at the beginning of the fermentation process and be part of the complete fermentation cycle. The only way to achieve this is as follows:

Equipment Needed

- Three small vessels that can hold approximately half a cupful of liquid with enough space to allow fermentation gases to expand
- Three and a half cups spring water
- One packet brewer's yeast
- One cup honey from a known organic source, not store bought
- Small saucepan for heating the water
- Three pieces of muslin and string to cover each vessel

Method

As this is quite a lengthy process because each flower component has to be fermented separately, we will craft all three simultaneously.

Arrange all three vessels in a way that they may be worked with easily. Place the deconstructed flower petals into one of the vessels. Do the same with the leaves and flower head.

Add the brewer's yeast to a half cup of warm water to activate it. Some fermentation yeasts may have different methods of activation. Please read and follow the manufacturer's instructions.

Place one cup of honey and three cups of water into a saucepan and heat to dissolve the honey. Do not boil the liquid. Allow to cool to room temperature.

Add the yeast solution to the dissolved honey and stir vigorously.

Pour enough of the honey-yeast solution into each vessel to cover the flower components to a depth of approximately half an inch. Shake each vessel to ensure all flower components are covered.

Cover each vessel with a double thickness of clean muslin and tie it in place. This allows the initial vigorous fermentation gases produced in the early stages of the process to escape while preventing any airborne bacteria from entering the vessel.

Place all three vessels in a warm place to facilitate the fermentation process. Return to the vessels each day and shake them to assist the process.

After one week, remove the muslin covers on all three vessels and replace with a loose-fitting stopper. Do not seal the vessels tightly at this stage. This will allow the remaining fermentation gases to escape. Leave to ferment for a further three weeks.

The vessels may then be sealed, or the fermented liquid, together with the flower components, may be transferred to smaller individual bottles where they may be stored until they are to be elevated and reunited to craft the final potion. Do not combine the individual cardinal essences until they are to be used.

Having explored the various forms of extracting the cardinal essences of flowers, we should now look to the flowers themselves and consider which flowers are best suited to each circumstance.

SIX

Crafting and Casting Potions

Before looking at the practical aspects of crafting flower magic potions, it is important that we examine and understand the principles underpinning their crafting and use, the most fundamental of these being the principle of the three cardinals, their separation, elevation, and their final reuniting, each stage of which is imperative in the crafting of any flower potion. We have explored the tenet of the three cardinals and how we separate each from its different location in the flower. We have also seen the various ways in which each of these individual cardinals may be extracted from its original flower component, leaving us with the crafted cardinal essence in the form of a liquid, syrup, powder, and so on. These various essences, although created as soon as possible after the flower was harvested, may be stored until they are intended to be used, and it is the next step of elevating these primary essences before reuniting them that we now need to explore.

The reason that we separate each component of the flower and extract its individual cardinal essence separately is that each represents a different aspect of the overall flower and as such each cardinal essence needs to be elevated in a different way. As noted in chapter 3, the three essences respectively represent: the universal (world) energy contained in the petals, which connects it to the universal natural energy that pervades all living things; the individual (personal) energy contained in the flower head, which identifies it as a unique species and as an individual flower; and the material (physical) energy contained in the leaves, which defines its manifestation as a flower within our physical world. As a result, each component requires a different form of elevation.

The purpose of the individual elevation is twofold: the first is to elevate the essence from the mundane to the spiritual, and the second is to amplify its unique spiritual energy as defined above. Once each individual cardinal essence has been elevated in a separate procedure, it is then necessary to reunite all three so that the eventual potion or elixir may reunify all the virtues and attributes of the original flower in the exact same balance as it appears in nature. This reuniting must take place as near as possible to the time the potion is to be used. It is imperative that the three elevated cardinal essences are all extracted from the individual components of the same flower and extracted and elevated at the same working. The concept of reuniting the cardinal essences is the same, no matter whether the carrier is liquid, syrup, or powder. The method and ritual of reuniting is explained in detail in the various examples shown below, as is the method of casting the potion in conjunction with the invocation of the planned intention.

LOVE PHILTERS

Love potions, more commonly known as philters, are, without doubt, the most popular type of potion that I am asked to craft as a practicing Druid. However, they are also the most misunderstood.

To understand how love philters influence the recipient, it is first necessary to appreciate how Druidic lore differentiates between emotional bonding and the physical aspects of sexual attraction. Love philters are intended to create an emotional bonding, and although this typically develops into a physical attraction, this aspect is not the original intention. Later, we will explore the types of potions that may be used to create attraction, enticement, and fascination, each of which focuses upon the physical and sexual characteristics of a relationship. It is necessary, therefore, to differentiate and separate these two aspects of what we may generally consider love. Importantly, the intention of physical and sexual desire can and must be isolated from the emotional attachment of love. The ultimate objective of physical and sexual attraction is to achieve the serene and intense orgasm that is the basic tenet of all sex magic. Without this separation, it would only be possible to undertake a sex magic ritual within the context of everyone who is involved being emotionally bonded with each other, which, of course, is very often not the case.

What follows are directions for crafting a Druidic love philter using a dog rose flower, from the beginning to the point where the philter is ready to play its part in the casting of the intention or spell. The crafting may be adapted and used for any suitable flower in exactly the same manner.

✤ Crafting a Love Philter from a Dog Rose Flower

We shall now look at each of the successive stages in crafting a flower love philter from a dog rose flower harvested from the wild. But before the crafting begins, we must consider if the application of a flower love philter is the best and most appropriate way to achieve the desired result.

When a person, in this example a female, is experiencing unrequited emotional love and is seeking to invoke a feeling of love in her intended partner, it would appear that a love philter is the perfect solution. However, serious consideration should be given to the ramifications of arousing such powerful emotions within the intended partner and how such feelings will affect his current lifestyle. Some practitioners assume a more committed responsibility in this consideration than others, and attitudes may range from assuming a personal responsibility for the more far-reaching impact of their spell casting to feeling that the responsibility lies entirely with the person requesting the potion. Experience suggests that a stance somewhere between the two extremes is the most likely to succeed in the long run. While it is irresponsible to ignore obvious pitfalls, such as the intended partner being married or not identifying as the gender intended, it is also unhelpful for the practitioner to be involved in the long-term, intimate details of any resultant relationship. It is for each practitioner to establish his own position and to be aware that this may also vary from circumstance to circumstance.

Assuming that the practitioner satisfied himself that a love philter is an appropriate intervention, then the wild dog rose is a suitable flower from which to craft a potion. As we shall now be looking at the details of crafting a love philter from the dog rose, this is an appropriate point to look at the plant in some detail. Some of this information may be repeated in the flower directory in chapter 10, but it is included here for the sake of completeness.

⤷ Dog rose (*Rosa canina*)

Irish: *feirdhris* (no translation)
Scottish: *dh 'èirich cù* (no translation)
Welsh: *rhosyn gwyllt* (wild rose)
Flowers: June to August

Other common names for the dog rose flower and its berries or hips (the name hip is most likely derived from the Anglo-Saxon *hiope,* meaning "berry or fruit") include: bird briar, briar rose, buckie berries, canker, canker berry, canker flower, canker rose, cat whin, choop tree, common briar, dogberry, dog briar, hep briar, hep rose, wild rose, rambling rose, and witches' briar. It is generally believed that the name dog rose came out of the belief that a remedy derived from the plant's root was a cure for the bite of a mad or rabid dog. Others suggest the name may be derived from the hooked prickles of the stem of the plant, which may resemble a dog's canine teeth.

The dog rose is a medium-size shrub with green foliage and pale pink or white flowers approximately five centimeters, or two inches, across, growing solitarily or in small clusters (see plate 2). It blooms in early spring, and small red fruit called rose hips follow the flower. Being deciduous, the plant loses all its leaves in autumn and fresh foliage appears again the following spring.

The hips of the dog rose, also known as rose haws, may range in color from bright red to a dark red approaching purple or black. The bright red hips appear from October to November and are rich in vitamin C. Each hip has a fleshy outer skin containing a hairy loose inner mass. In most uses the inner hairy mass is removed, leaving the red outer flesh, which may be used to craft infusions, syrups, and other potions. Over the years there have been a wide variety of cures and syrups manufactured from the hips used to treat common colds, flu, and other ailments that may benefit from an intake of vitamin C. The rosy flesh of the dog rose hip is used extensively in crafting *rhodomel,* meaning "rose-honey," a type of short-mead used in many Druidic workings and rituals. The fine hairy seeds in the hip's core are often used by children who place them down the backs of their friends where they irritate the skin. These "itchy bugs" are a common itching powder with the youngsters of Wales, Scotland, Ireland, and the rest of the British Isles.

During much of the fifteenth century, most of Britain was preoccupied with the English Civil War, a bitter conflict over the control of the throne of England. Both rival armies adopted a rose as their emblem: the House of Lancaster represented by the red rose and the House of York represented by the white dog rose. As result, this series of civil conflicts became known as the Wars of the Roses and eventually ended in the complete elimination of both male lines of the disputed House of Plantagenet, leading to the end of the Plantagenet reign and the rise of the Tudor dynasty in England. Even so, the rose remains the national flower of England, where there are fourteen native wild varieties. The flower or its hips appear on a variety of heraldic devices throughout Europe, and, it became a popular image in medieval folklore. It remains the adopted county flower of Hampshire in England and of County Leitrim in Ireland, which has subsequently become known as the Wild Rose County as a result of the plants' abundance in the hedgerows and fields of the region.

The dog rose has been associated with magical practices since prehistory, and there are many accounts of its use in traditional witchcraft, where it is held to contain powers of luck, protection, and healing, along with its widely held association with love. In Druidic flower magic, the dog rose holds a wide range of magical properties; in fact, it is one of the most versatile flowers native to the shores of Britain and Ireland. It is included in a large variety of cures and remedies in addition to its potent spiritual applications. Its most powerful virtues are employed in workings that influence good fortune, happiness, and friendly relations.

It is therefore commonly utilized in attraction potions, workings designed to resolve conflict, and those designed to engender protection, well-being, and contentment. Potions produced from the dog rose are frequently employed in magical workings intended for females and would be employed to increase confidence, celebrate beauty, and increase female intuition, sensuality, and emotional love. Importantly, potions derived from the dog rose are also used in workings related to truthfulness. Workings that reveal the truth, expose untruths, or secure the truth all employ dog rose flower potions.

Most famously, the dog rose flower is associated with love workings, where the philter crafted from the flower is used to attract love and bind long lasting love. In contrast, potions using the flower and thorns are used to deter unwanted love, turn away unwanted admirers, and expose infidelity. The sharp spiky thorns that cover the dog rose branches are also used in workings that invoke protection, while the same thorns are used in witchcraft dark magic to induce pain and suffering in the intended victim—they are used to impale small physical effigies of the victim called poppets in a way similar to voodoo doll magic. Casting the petals of the dog rose at malevolent witches distracts them from their unpleasant work as they become preoccupied in counting the flower petals, forgetting their witchcraft and curses.

Identifying, Harvesting, and Maintaining the Flower

The first practical stage in crafting a flower potion using the dog rose is the identification of an appropriate individual flower from which the philter is to be crafted. Previously, we have looked at the various aspects that may influence the properties of an individual flower, such as the influence of a neighboring plant(s), the terroir in which the individual plant has grown, the age of the plant, and so on, and I refer the reader to chapter 4. An example of a suitable dog rose flower can be found, within the grounds of Monmouth Castle in East Wales, where, a small community of dog roses grows surrounded by a grassy verge, effectively isolating the group from other external influences and intensifying its virtues.

The harvesting of the flower is the next consideration. As the eventual philter is to be cast upon a male, then the flower is best harvested in the early morning sunshine, when it is not raining or affected by any other adverse weather conditions. Remembering that the philter must be crafted from the component parts of the plant in the proportion that they appear in nature, the harvester counts the petals on the flower and ensures that the same number of leaves are harvested from the flower stalk. In the case of the dog rose, this is particularly easy as the leaves grow in groups of five on a single stalk, the same number as there are petals on the flower. The single flower head is pinched from its stalk between the finger and thumb, as close to the base of the flower head as possible.

Maintaining the flower's integrity until it is crafted is essential, as it is very rarely that the philter is crafted in the same location from which the flower is harvested. Typically the freshly harvested flower and leaves are carefully wrapped in a damp paper towel to transport them to the practitioner's workshop. Great care must be taken to ensure the flower head is not crushed or bruised during its journey. When convenient, the flower head and leafstalk may be placed in a bowl of water to help maintain their freshness, but if the harvesting and crafting are planned correctly, the philter will be crafted very soon after the flower is harvested.

Deconstructing the Flower Head

After the practitioner has cast a protective circle and cleansed its interior, the crafting working may begin. (See instructions for casting a protective circle on page 50.) The first stage in the working is deconstructing the flower head and the leafstalk. In relation to this working, the dog rose flower head is made up of two principal component parts, the five petals and the remaining flower head, which, importantly, contains the reproductive elements of the flower. Each petal is carefully removed from the flower head by pulling it away gently while holding it between the finger and thumb. They are never cut off the flower head, as this would be an unnatural separation. It should be remembered that in its natural habitat, the petals fall from the flower head as it decomposes, and it is this action that the practitioner attempts to emulate. Each of the five petals is placed aside as it is separated until all five are removed. The remaining flower head is placed aside with the petals. The five corresponding leaves are then removed from their stalk by pinching them between the finger and thumb, as close as possible to the main stalk itself, while leaving the short leafstalk remaining at the base of each leaf. When all five have been removed, the main stalk is retained so that it may be returned to the location of its harvesting and placed among the plant community. At this point, we now have the three individual flower components from which we intend to extract the cardinal essences (see plate 3).

Extracting and Storing the Cardinal Essences

In chapter 5, we looked at the process of extracting the three cardinal essences as a general process and working. Here we will focus on the extraction of the cardinal essences from the three component parts of the dog rose by means of cold water maceration as part of the crafting of a love philter.

Each of the three individual flower components is placed in a separate small vessel and covered with sufficient solvent to cover it completely. In this case, the flower components are macerated in cold spring water. Each vessel is then tightly sealed and placed in a position where it will be exposed to direct sunlight and moonlight for a period of seven days to allow the solvent spring water to absorb the virtues and attributes of the dog rose components (see plate 4).

Following this sun and moon energizing and the absorption of the dog rose attributes, the individual cardinal essences, as they may now be called, are stored until they are to be used. Storing the individual cardinal essences may be done in a cool, dark place, for any period up to six months. During this storage time the component parts remain in the solvent; it should be noted that storing the cardinal essences does not increase the potency of the essences, but if done correctly, it will not reduce their potency either. When the final potion is to be crafted, the three vessels containing the essences are retrieved so that they may be individually elevated as the next stage in the crafting.

Elevating the Cardinal Essences

Elevating the cardinal essences is the process whereby the spiritual virtues of the cardinal essences are amplified, increased by ritual working from the mundane to the nonphysical. This is achieved by a simple yet profound Druidic rite. This rite or working is performed on a working stone enclosed within a protective circle that prevents any negative energies that may be present from affecting the virtues of the flower's essences. Before sealing the circle, the practitioner ensures all the equipment needed for elevating the three cardinal essences is placed on the working stone (three vials and cold spring water), along with the practitioner's wand, a small ceramic bowl, preferably with a spout to facilitate pouring the essence back into its original small bottle, and a clean linen cloth.

The bottle containing the first of the cardinal essences is placed in front of the ceramic bowl. The wand is energized (see below) and placed on top of the ceramic bowl at the center of the working stone. Before beginning the working, the practitioner must clear her thoughts and spend a moment focusing upon the task ahead, visualizing each of the steps that follow repeatedly until she is confident that the entire working is clear to her.

Empowering the Wand

The first step in the elevation working is to empower or potentialize the wand. This is achieved in the same way no matter what the wand's intended working or use may be. To begin, the wand is held in the dominant hand. The practitioner then focuses on converging his personal energy into the wand. This is achieved by visualizing the energy residing in each part of his body being transferred to the wand. First, the energy residing within the practitioner's mind is visualized, bundled, and mobilized as it begins its journey to the wand. It is visualized as being "parked" at the base of the skull at the back of the neck where it waits to be united with the energy from the rest of the body.

Most practitioners would now focus the same intention on their right leg, and beginning with the tip of the toes gather the energies residing there, and then add to it the other energies at the ankle, knee, hip, and spine as they move the growing bundle to join the parked energy at the base of the skull, where they are bound together. This gathering process is repeated for the other leg, then each hand and arm, the abdomen, and the thorax, until all the vital energies of the body converge at the skull base. This accumulated personal energy is then transposed through the shoulder along the dominant arm and hand until it is deposited within the wand. By this means we maximize the potential energy lying latent within the body, gather it, and transfer it to the wand. The energized wand is then placed on top of the ceramic bowl at the center of the working stone.

The small bottle containing the first of the cardinal essences is then held in both hands and raised high above the stone. Focusing upon the bottle, the practitioner says:

> *This essence has been extracted from the dog rose flower with all the care and knowledge inherited from my Druidic ancestors. I call upon the whole of nature to empower this essence and this working, as it has done since the beginning of time.*

The bottle is then lowered, and its cork removed. The liquid is gently poured over the wand so that it drips into the ceramic bowl below. As the liquid flows over the wand, it is energized by the wand itself as it also absorbs the personal energy of the practitioner previously invested within. When all of the essence has been poured from the bottle, it is placed aside as the liquid is allowed to drip from the wand for a few more moments. The wand is then removed from the top of the bowl. The elevated essence is carefully poured back into its original bottle, which is then resealed and aside until it is to be reunited in the next stage of the working. The empty ceramic bowl and the wand are then wiped clean and dried with the linen cloth.

This same process is repeated for the remaining two cardinal essences so that all three are elevated in the same way. The wand need not be reenergized for each essence as the personal energy invested within it is more than sufficient for the entire working. Once all three cardinal essences have been elevated, they stand ready to be reunited to form the final flower potion.

Reuniting the Cardinal Essences

The final stage in crafting the love philter is the reuniting of the three individual cardinal essences. This is typically done immediately following the elevation described above. This being the case, the same working stone may be used as it remains within the sealed protective circle. To achieve this final crafting, the practitioner will need all three elevated cardinal essences, the same ceramic bowl (cleaned and dried), the practitioner's wand (already energized from the previous working), a small bottle to contain the philter, and a dark cloth or pouch with which to wrap the philter to protect it from exposure to the light.

The working begins by placing the ceramic bowl at the front and center of the working stone. The cardinal essence from each small bottle is then poured into the bowl so that they mingle. (It is important that the flower material in each essence remains in its bottle and that following the working it is returned to the location where it was initially harvested, returned to the ground with a brief invocation of thanks.) The combined cardinal essences are then slowly stirred with the wand as a reuniting invocation is spoken. This invocation may (remembering this philter is crafted for a female to cast upon a male) typically be:

> *By reuniting these cardinal essences I bring together*
> *the spiritual energies of the dog rose and its virtues of*
> *arousing and binding emotional love. May this philter*
> *invoke the deepest and most potent love between the*
> *woman who casts it and the man who will receive it.*

When the practitioner is confident that the philter is successfully coalesced, the wand is placed aside and the finished philter is carefully poured into the small bottle and tightly sealed. The sealed bottle is then wrapped in the dark cloth or placed in the pouch to protect it from sunlight until it is to be cast.

Casting the Potion

Casting the potion along with the intention requires the person casting the intention to be in close proximity to the recipient upon whom the intention is to be cast. It is important to note that the person casting the intention is rarely the practitioner who crafted it, but usually the person who is attempting to instill a loving emotion in the person upon whom the intention is being cast. In other words, the philter and its accompanying intention are cast upon the person to make him love the person who cast it. This being the case, the person casting the philter must be given precise instructions on how the philter is to be cast, what the result will be, and the pitfalls and dangers of casting it improperly. Emotional love is a powerful and profound emotion and therefore requires a considered and responsible approach. The ramifications of the improper use of love philters are far reaching, extremely dangerous, and may, in extreme cases, result in physical and/or mental damage to all parties involved. It is the practitioner's responsibility to ensure that the individual casting the intention is aware of all the potential dangers and difficulties and that he fully understands the practical stages of casting the philter.

In order for the philter and its accompanying intention to effectively bind itself to the recipient, two events must occur simultaneously: the philter must come into direct contact with the recipient's body, and the casting intention must be spoken at the moment of contact. Typically, the liquid philter is dripped onto the recipient's skin from its bottle, and it must be noted that *no* philters are crafted to be drunk; in fact, most would induce serious ill effects if they are ingested. The means of casting the philter to the recipient's skin will vary and mainly depends upon whether the recipient is cooperating with the working or if it is being done without the recipient's knowledge. If the recipient is unaware of the casting, then it is up to the caster's ingenuity to contrive a circumstance where a philter may be dropped upon the recipient's skin. If the recipient is aware of the casting, then a suitable method to apply the philter may be agreed upon between the caster and the recipient. Either way, it is important to recognize that it is sufficient to apply any amount of the philter to the recipient, no matter how small—even a single, small drop will attain results, as each minute atom of the philter contains the complete attributes of the chosen flower and has the same effect as using the complete philter. This is one of the reasons why even a single small flower may be used in Druidic flower magic.

To complete the casting, the caster must memorize the intention to be invoked as the philter is cast. Typically, this may be:

> I cast upon you this potion of love. May it invoke
> within you the primal emotion of love, direct it and
> bind it to me in an everlasting bond. I do this within
> the auspices of the natural magic of my ancestors and
> the communal spirit of the universe.

This intention may be spoken loudly, whispered quietly, or even simply repeated silently within the caster's mind. What is important is that it is invoked exactly as the philter is cast upon the recipient's skin and that it is invoked with sincerity, understanding the provenance and responsibility of casting such an intention. On most occasions, the philter is cast directly from the bottle in which it has been held, but this is not always the case. Alternatively, a specific magic device may be used to cast the philter, and a range of these is discussed later in the chapter.

As well as using philters as a means of inducing and binding emotional love, other potions crafted from the cardinal essences of selected flowers may be used in a wide range of potions to achieve other, equally important objectives. In each case, the sequence of crafting the potion follows the same path. The next potions we shall explore are those used to invoke attraction and fascination.

ATTRACTION, FASCINATION, AND GLAMOURS

It may not always be the case that it is another person that one wants to attract; often it may be an object, a change, or a circumstance, like money or a new home, or even a new feeling, such as attracting happiness or increased energy. None of these things can be attracted by using the love philter previously discussed, so another potion and invocation must be employed. As some of these desires are not necessarily physical items or individuals, there are difficulties in using some of the techniques we have looked at previously as an attraction device, as there is no way to literally touch them to the desired target, so a method of casting and binding the intention to a concept rather than an object or person must be employed.

Attraction working may be used to draw things or concepts to a person while glamours are workings used to instill a fascination between two individuals (different from instilling love with a philter) to encourage friendship and bonding, even within a family or group. Fortunately, both intentions may be achieved through very similar workings, requiring the same magical devices, potions, and ritual.

೪ Crafting an Attraction Potion from a Meadow Buttercup Flower

Here, we will focus on an attraction working employed with the intention of attracting good fortune to a family home. In this specific example, we shall look at crafting an attraction potion within a protective circle and then casting this potion and intention inside the home using a hook wand as its principal magical device. The potion will be crafted from the meadow buttercup flower, steeped in hot spring water. The wild meadow buttercup has been chosen as, in addition to its virtue of prophecy, it is well known as a flower of attraction and binding. While associated with the sun (because of its brilliant golden yellow color), it is also considered to have the attributes of good fortune and wealth. Before beginning the potion crafting, it will be useful to explore the meadow buttercup in detail.

⟫ Buttercup, meadow (*Ranunculus acris*)

Irish: *fearbán féir* (grassy buttercup)
Scottish: *buidheag-an-t-samhraidh* (little yellow of the summer)
Welsh: *blodyn ymenyn* (butter flower)
Flowers: May to August

The meadow buttercup is a common wild plant and can be found growing on waysides, in ditches, and among open fields. The flower has five shiny yellow petals (see plate 5). The leaves are triangular with three lobes and covered with fine hairs. At the base of each petal is tiny cup-shaped scale containing the flower's nectar, which attracts bees, and it is this minute cup of nectar that gives the buttercup its name along with its virtue of attraction. In the Welsh Druidic tradition, buttercups are held to be a beneficent plant, particularly among ancient dairy farmers, who associated the yellow color of the flower with fine butter and wholesome eggs. It remains a tradition among the rural farmers of Wales to rub their dairy cows' udders with buttercup flowers to ensure the richness of their milk and to protect them from the fairies. In the same way, young children have long placed a buttercup flower under each other's chins, and if the yellow color is reflected on the underside of the chin, then that child is said to like butter. It is also part of the rural Welsh tradition that swallows feed their young on buttercup flowers, giving them prophetic abilities and far-reaching sight.

Note, however, that buttercups are toxic, and potions crafted from them are never, ever to be ingested.

Identifying, Harvesting, and Deconstructing a Meadow Buttercup

In crafting an attraction potion from a meadow buttercup steeped in hot spring water, the first practical stage is the identification of an appropriate individual meadow buttercup flower. This is done using the same criteria described under the dog rose potion. Once an individual flower has been identified, it is harvested by the same means and method described previously and then maintained in the same manner discussed until it is to be crafted.

The first stage in the working is deconstructing the flower head and the leafstalk. The meadow buttercup flower head is made up of two component parts, the petals and the remaining flower head, which importantly contains the reproductive elements of the flower. The deconstruction methodology has been explained previously and once completed leaves us with five individual flower petals, the flower head, and individual leaves (the same number as there are petals), all prepared for the next stage of the working (see plate 6).

Extracting and Storing the Cardinal Essences

The process of extracting the three cardinal essences from the three component parts of the meadow buttercup is achieved in this example by steeping the parts in hot spring water.

For this particular working the practitioner will need three small heat-proof bowls, a jug containing hot spring water, and a ladle (optional), together with the three component parts of the meadow buttercup that have previously been separated in the deconstruction working.

To begin, the petals are placed in one of the small bowls and immediately covered with the hot spring water from the jug, either by pouring directly from the jug or using the ladle to transfer the water (see plate 7). The same is then done in separate bowls with the flower head and the leaves.

The contents of all three bowls are then left to cool, during which time the spring water absorbs the virtues of the meadow buttercup. When at room temperature, the spring water and flower material from each bowl is transferred to three individual small bottles, which are then tightly sealed.

They are then placed in a location where they are directly exposed to the sunlight and the moonlight for a minimum of six days to allow the liquid to continue to absorb the virtues of the meadow buttercup flower. Following this sun and moon energizing, the three bottles containing the cardinal essences are stored in a cool, dark place until they are to be used. These cardinal essences may be stored in this way for up to six months. When the final potion is to be crafted, the three vessels containing the essences are retrieved so that they may be individually elevated as the next stage in the crafting.

Elevating the Cardinal Essences

Elevating the cardinal essences amplifies their physical and spiritual energies prior to their reuniting. As before, elevating the cardinal essences of the flower is conducted at a working stone enclosed in a protective circle of sea salt (see page 50 for instructions). In this working the practitioner will need to place upon the working stone all three bottles containing the cardinal essences of the meadow buttercup; a ceramic bowl, preferably with a spout, to receive each essence as it is elevated; a clean linen cloth to clean the bowl between each of the three elevations; and a suitable wand to elevate the essences. (See the section on the next page, "Crafting a Hook Wand.")

Within the protective circle, the practitioner begins the working by raising the wand high and then slowly and reverentially speaking an invocation of the practitioner's own composition, which may be similar to:

> *Now that this wand has been harvested and thanks*
> *has been spoken to its donor, I seek to free it of all*
> *unwanted influences and elevate its inherent energies*
> *and virtues so that it may aid me in my working.*

This continues until the practitioner is confident that the wand is ready to be used in the attraction working. This may be done just prior to the elevation of the cardinal essences, in which case the same protective circle is used. If this is not the case, then the hook wand may be put aside until it is needed. However, it is important that the hook wand is used within as short a time as possible in order to utilize its maximum potential.

To begin the working, the practitioner places the ceramic bowl at the center of the working stone and lays the energized hook wand across the top of the bowl. The small bottle containing the first of the cardinal essences is then held in both hands and raised high above the stone. Focusing upon the bottle, the practitioner says:

This essence has been extracted from the meadow buttercup flower with all the care and knowledge inherited from my Druidic ancestors. I call upon the whole of nature to empower this essence and this working, as it has done since the beginning of time.

The bottle is then lowered and its cork removed. The liquid is then gently poured over the hook wand so that it drips into the ceramic bowl below. As the liquid flows over the hook wand, it is energized by the wand itself as it also absorbs the personal energy of the practitioner previously invested within the wand. When all of the essence has been poured from the bottle, it is placed aside as the liquid is allowed to drip from the wand for a few more moments. The wand is then removed from the top of the bowl. The elevated essence is carefully poured back into its original bottle, which is then resealed and set aside until it is to be reunited in the next stage of the working. The empty ceramic bowl and the hook wand are then wiped clean and dried with the linen cloth.

This same process is repeated for the remaining two cardinal essences so that all three are elevated in the same way. The wand need not be reenergized for each essence as the personal energy invested within it is more than sufficient for the entire working. Once this is complete, all three cardinal essences have been elevated and stand ready to be reunited to form the final flower potion.

Crafting a Hook Wand

A hook wand is typically used when the intention is to gather things, thoughts, or emotions toward the person casting a spell or philter. For this reason, a hook wand is used for the meadow buttercup attraction potion. The wand needs to be hook shaped in appearance and used in a hooking motion, drawing the intention toward the caster. The most appropriate tree species for crafting wands for attraction invocations are the oak (due to its wisdom and longevity), the rowan (a tree of attraction, other than to witches and sorcerers), and the sycamore (another tree of attraction and binding).

Here, we will learn how to craft a hook wand from a blood-thorn briar branch with one remaining thorn at its tip acting as the hooking element of the wand (see plate 8). A blood-thorn is a particular briar that, due to the terroir in which it has grown, presents blood-red thorns on a green branch. Such thorns are rare and hold a special place in Druidic tradition. They have many uses, among them creating a protection potion by placing a single thorn in a bottle of mead (see plate 9); this potion is detailed in chapter 7.

The first thing to note is that *all* Druidic wands are crafted from living trees or plants and are only effective while they are still living. Such living wands are never left to dry, harden, or mature but must be used while they still contain the living sap of the plant from which they are harvested. The wand is crafted by harvesting a blood-thorn branch approximately eighteen inches long and then removing all the individual leaves and thorns along its length except for one thorn, which remains at the tip of the wand with the thorn curved toward the practitioner. This enables the wand to be used in a hooking motion, drawing or attracting the target of the invocation toward the practitioner, if the intention is to draw the target toward the practitioner. If such a working is intended to attract the target toward another person, then the practitioner will need to instruct that person to undertake the working effectively.

As we have seen before, an invocation of thanksgiving is spoken as the branch is harvested and any small twigs and leaves are trimmed and left at the foot of the donor briar.

Once the hook wand has been harvested, its shape is refined in the practitioner's workshop, and the heel end of the wand, opposite the tip, is cut at a diagonal so that the maximum surface area of its core may be brought in contact with the practitioner's palm when the intention is being cast and bound. Again, like all other living wands, the hook wand is crafted for a single specific purpose and must be used while all the living sap and vitality is still held within the branch.

After the hook wand has been cut and shaped, it must now be

potentialized, used for its desired purpose, and then returned to nature at the location where it was harvested. The hook wand is potentialized within a protective circle that has been closed, sealed, and cleansed. The working is done at the working stone and, as with other wands, it begins with the wand being energized and empowered. Energizing amplifies and liberates the wand's inherent attributes and vitality, while empowerment imbues the wand with the specific spiritual energies of the practitioner, giving it the potential to project and bind the intention to its recipient or objective.

When there is a need for a particularly powerful attraction working, consideration should be given to using an ivy-entwined hook wand, whereby the blood-thorn wand is wound around with a length of ivy, which in itself has enormous attraction and binding energies. In this case, the wand is wrapped or entwined within the protective circle prior to its potentializing.

Reuniting the Cardinal Essences

The final stage in crafting the potion is the reuniting of the three individual cardinal essences to form the eventual attraction potion. This is typically done immediately following the elevation working described above, and the same working stone may be used as it remains within the sealed protective circle. To achieve this final crafting, the practitioner will need all three elevated cardinal essences, the same ceramic bowl (cleaned and dried), the hook wand (already energized from the previous working), a small bottle to contain the finished potion, and a dark cloth or pouch with which to wrap the potion to protect it from exposure to the light.

The working begins by once again placing the ceramic bowl at the front and center of the working stone. The cardinal essence from each small bottle is then poured into the bowl so that they mingle. It is important that the flower material in each essence remains in its bottle and that following the working each is returned to the location where it was initially harvested and returned to the ground with a brief invocation of thanks. The combined cardinal essences are then slowly stirred with the wand as a reuniting invocation is spoken. A typical invocation is:

> *By reuniting these cardinal essences, I bring together the spiritual energies of the meadow buttercup and its virtues. May this potion bring to its caster the most potent attraction and bonding.*

When the practitioner is confident that the potion is successfully coalesced, the wand is placed aside and the finished potion is carefully poured into the small bottle and tightly sealed. The sealed bottle is then wrapped in the dark cloth or placed in the pouch to protect it from sunlight until it is to be cast.

Casting the Potion

As this example is one of an attracting intention, the casting of the potion along with the intention has to be achieved without the person necessarily being in close proximity to the receiving person, place, object, or circumstance. It is important to note that the person casting the intention is rarely the practitioner who crafted it, but usually the person who is attempting to attract the desired object, person, or so on to him. In other words, the potion and its accompanying intention is cast remotely from the desired object in order to attract it to the person casting the intention. This being the case, the person casting the potion must be given precise instructions on how the potion and intention are to be cast, what the intended result will be, and the pitfalls and dangers of casting it improperly. It is therefore the practitioner's responsibility to ensure that the individual casting the intention is aware of all the potential dangers and difficulties involved and that he fully understands the practical stages of casting the potion and its intention. In order for the potion and its accompanying intention to effectively bind itself to the recipient, two events must occur simultaneously: the potion must be cast toward the recipient person, object, or so on using the hook wand as a magic device, and the casting intention must be spoken at the moment of casting.

This casting working differs significantly from the example we saw earlier, in that the casting of the potion is not done with the aim of the potion coming into contact with the recipient directly, but with the objective of inducing the conveyance of the intention through the universal energy to the recipient, thereby attracting it or them to the person casting it. As noted, this example is one of attracting good fortune to a family home.

For the purpose of this illustration, the practitioner has chosen to conduct the attraction working from within the family home. In this instance, there is no need to construct a protective circle as the working is intended to attract good fortune to the home as a whole. However, the practitioner will need a working stone (e.g., a wooden table) upon which to conduct the working, the reunited potion, a small ceramic bowl, and the blood-thorn hook wand. On occasion, the practitioner may also choose to place two lit candles at the front of the working stone, as this may be helpful in illuminating the way for the attracted intention.

The ceramic bowl is placed at the center of the working stone. Before beginning the physical casting of the potion, the practitioner must focus his concentration upon the process of the working. In this instance this means visualizing a source of good fortune residing within the universal energy. This may be a ball of light, a cloud of a particular color, a cave containing a deposit of good fortune, or any similar visualization that the practitioner may imagine. The reason for this is that although we know that good fortune, like its opposite, bad fortune, resides universally within the world spirit, but in order to attract this fortuitous energy it must be envisaged as a single source. The practitioner then continues to visualize the pending working by attaching to that good fortune source any form of capture. Typically this may be a tether to tie around it, a bottle in which it may be sealed, or a casket in which it may be secured. The captured energy is then visualized as undertaking a journey from its source to where it is to be bound, in this case, from its source to the house of the requesting family. When the visualized captured energy arrives at the destination, it is bound securely to it so that its energy may percolate throughout its new location. This then represents the capturing, attraction, journey, and binding of the good fortune energy to its desired new location and is, of course, the entire purpose of the working. The reason for this rehearsal is that, like all Druidic workings, this casting should not begin until the entire process and its outcome is completely understood and memorized. The practitioner may choose to repeat this visualization any number of times, but certainly until he is confident that the entire working is firmly embedded in memory. Once the practitioner is prepared in this way, the practical elements of the working may begin.

The practitioner first pours the reunited potion from its bottle into the ceramic bowl. The tip of the hook wand is dipped into the potion and raised into the air and the liquid potion is flicked to the first of the compass directions, north. While doing this, the practitioner speaks an invocation, which may be similar to:

> *I cast this potion to the north in the knowledge that it*
> *will find its way to the source of the energy I seek.*

In doing this, the practitioner visualizes the potion reaching the source of the good fortune as visualized earlier. The same casting and invocation is then cast to each of the principal compass points in turn: east, south, then west. This intention may be spoken loudly, whispered quietly, or even simply repeated silently within the caster's mind. Here we see the hook wand being used in the form of an aspergillum or aspergil, casting empowered liquid toward its recipient. Next, the hook wand is used as a hook, drawing the good fortune energy toward the home. This is achieved by the practitioner facing north and raising the hook wand to eye level and then moving the wand in such a way as it hooks the energy described above. This hooking action is repeated as the practitioner declaims:

> *I draw to this place the energy I seek.*

This action is once again repeated toward each successive compass point as before. While doing this, the practitioner visualizes the captured energy moving toward its destination, following its journey as it took place during the rehearsal visualization. Once the practitioner is confident that the energy is present at the home, he then dips the wand tip into the potion once again and flicks the liquid in the direction of the north while saying:

I bind this energy to this place and banish any negative forces from influencing it.

This is repeated again for each of the other major compass points, east, south, and west. In doing this, the practitioner visualizes the energy source (however originally visualized) permeating the fabric of the home and being bound there in perpetuity. At this point the working is complete, and all that is left to do is return both the remaining potion and the used hook wand to their original harvest location and restore them to nature with a brief invocation of thanks.

SEX MAGIC POTIONS AND CONJURATIONS

We have considered the differences between a love philter and whatever potions may be employed in sex magic workings and related conjurations. In doing so, we established that love philters act exclusively on the emotional aspects of love and attraction, and while this emotional element frequently develops into physical attraction, each of these facets must be considered as separate and independent, until such time as they are knowingly bound together. Earlier, we explored love philters used to invoke emotional feeling in their recipients, then we looked at how other feelings and influences may be attracted by using attraction potions (our example was of a potion used to attract good fortune). Now we shall explore how crafted potions may be used to influence physical attraction alone, through the concept of sex magic, where physical arousal is used, independent of emotional attachment, in order to cast and bind the practitioner's intentions.

ᦸ Crafting a Sex Magic Potion from a Dandelion Flower

In the example that follows we will see how a sex magic potion is used to enhance a sex magic working intended to project an intention using the power of a controlled orgasm as a means of projection and binding.

As with all Druidic sex magic workings, the first step is to identify the purpose of the working and if a sex magic working is the most appropriate means of achieving the desired outcome. The most important factor to remember here is that the Druidic sex magic working is not intended to be used for matters relating to sex or physical attraction, but rather that the sexual act promotes an orgasm, and it is this powerful energy, arguably humankind's most powerful energy, that is used exclusively as a force for the projection and binding of *any* intention, no matter what its intended outcome may be. It is this aspect of sex magic that makes the potion crafted and used in these workings unique, in as much as they are used as a means of intensifying and amplifying the sexual orgasm and not intended to influence the eventual recipient. In other words, the benefactor of the potion is the person who is casting the intention (using the power of her orgasm) and not the recipient of the desired outcome directly.

With this in mind, before deciding to use sex magic as a means of achieving the desired outcome, the practitioner must be confident that the outcome requires the most powerful means of casting possible. This may be appropriate if the recipient is a very long way from the casting; if it seems that casting and binding the intention are going to be opposed by other external influences or energies; if the desired result means a massive change or reversal in a well-established situation; or if the practitioner recognizes that there is no other means powerful enough to achieve the desired outcome effectively. If circumstances dictate that, for whatever reason, a sex magic working is the most appropriate action and that it would be desirable to enhance this working with the use of a flower potion, then the next step is to select the flower to be used to craft the required potion.

For the purpose of this example, we will assume that the desired outcome is to remove an existing curse from an elderly lady who is suffering constant misfortune and illness. Such curse spells are occasionally the currency of malicious cunning folk steeped in the knowledge of natural magic and the old ways of the forest. Remember, though, that the recipient of the potion is not the unfortunate old lady but the individual who will be casting the intention to remove the curse and restore the old lady's good fortune and good health. So the intended recipient of the crafted potion is a female Druid, who will be casting the intention using a sex magic working, and the intended outcome of the potion is to increase and amplify the work of the female Druid and not affect the old lady directly; she will, however, benefit indirectly by the amplifying of the female Druid's working.

To select the most appropriate flower potion, we must choose a flower that is most effectively used by a female and whose intention is to amplify the effect of a magic working. The best-suited flower to meet both of these criteria is the dandelion flower, as we will see from the following.

⤛ Dandelion (*Taraxacum officinale*)

Irish: *bior na bríde* (lance of the maiden)
Scottish: *fiacal leomhann* (lion's tooth)
Welsh: *dant y llew* (tooth of the lion)
Flowers: March to October

The leaves of the plant are serrated along their edges, and it is their appearance that gives rise to the flower's common name: dandelion, from the French *dents de lion* (lion's teeth). Other common folklore names for the dandelion include:

Welsh

Blodyn faint 'dy'r gloch (what-time-is-it flower)
Blodyn crach (scab flower)
Blodyn crafu (itchy flower)
Blodyn pi-pi gwely (pee pee the flowerbed)
Blodyn piso'n y gwely (piss in the flowerbed)
Dail clais (leaves of a bruise)
Dant y ci (tooth of the dog)

Irish

Beárnach (indented little gap)

Beárnán beárnaigh (little gap of the indented one)

The dandelion is a common wild plant and can be found growing on waysides, in open fields, and in grasslands. It has long had a reputation as a diuretic, and among its many uses is the flower's ability to help heal bruises. The dandelion differs from many other flowers used in Druidic flower magic in as much as it does not have actual petals; instead, it has a display of thin, bright yellow florets (see plate 10). The florets radiate from the center of the flower head and open in response to sunlight but close tightly again in overcast, cloudy weather and at nighttime. The florets develop into spheres of individual white parachutes, each holding a seed. These fairy spheres are well known to British children as dandelion clocks or Jenny Joes and are used in a number of children's games.

Identifying, Harvesting, and Deconstructing the Flower Head

In crafting an empowerment potion from a dandelion steeped in hazelnut oil, the first practical stage is the identification of an appropriate individual dandelion flower; this is done using the same criteria described earlier in the chapter.

Once an individual flower has been identified it is harvested by the same means and method described previously. One major consideration applicable to this specific working is that the potion is to be used to anoint a female, therefore it is important that it is harvested by moonlight and either used to craft the potion the same night or kept away from sunlight until it is to be used. Apart from this consideration, the flower and its leaves are then maintained in the same manner as detailed until it is to be crafted. The crafting of the empowerment potion begins with the casting, cleansing, and sealing of a protective circle, with the working stone sealed inside, as described previously.

The first stage in the working is deconstructing the flower head and the leafstalk. The dandelion flower head is made up of two principal component parts: its many radial florets and the remaining flower head, which importantly contains the reproductive elements of the flower. It is worth pointing out here that the ratio of florets to leaves differs from the standard rule. In the case of the dandelion, each flower stalk grows from ground level with its own group of leaves; in order to maintain the natural balance of the plant, the ratio of petals to leaves, which in other cases is one to one, changes to the total number of petals on the flower together with the total number of leaves on the individual stalk. The completed deconstruction leaves us with a collection of the many florets removed from the flower, the remaining central flower head, and the leaves growing on the single flower stalk, each prepared for the next stage of the working.

Extracting and Storing the Cardinal Essences

As the potion we are preparing to craft is to be used in a sex magic working, the extraction of its cardinal essences is to be done using the oil maceration process, leaving us with an eventual potion that may be massaged directly into the female Druid's skin. In this example we will use hazelnut oil, harvested and pressed by the practitioner herself. As with all products of the hazel tree, its oil has the virtues of wisdom and empowerment, ideal for this intended empowerment working.

The process of extracting the cardinal essences from each of the three component parts of the dandelion by means of steeping them in oil requires two small bowls or similar vessels, a larger, sealable bottle or jar to contain the flower's leaves, which may be too large to macerate in the small bowls, a measure of room- or body-temperature hazelnut oil, and, of course, the three separated components of the dandelion flower.

The dandelion florets are placed into one of the small bowls and the flower head in the other; the flower's leaves are placed into the small bottle. The hazelnut oil is then poured into each vessel in turn, covering the flower components completely (see plate 11).

All three vessels are then placed in a position where they will be exposed to direct sunlight and moonlight for a period of seven days to allow the solvent hazelnut oil to absorb the virtues and attributes of the dandelion components.

Following this sun and moon energizing and the absorption of the dandelion attributes, the individual cardinal essences, as they may now be called, are stored until they are to be used. In order to do this, the two essences held in the bowls are poured into small bottles and, along with the leaf essence, all three bottles are sealed tightly. The individual cardinal essences may be stored in a cool, dark place for up to six months. During this storage time, the component parts remain in the hazelnut oil solvent, but it should be noted that storing the cardinal essences does not increase the potency of the essences; if done correctly, it will not reduce their potency either. When the final potion is to be crafted, the three vessels containing the essences are retrieved so that they may be individually elevated during the next stage in the crafting.

Elevating the Cardinal Essences

Elevating the cardinal essences amplifies their physical and spiritual energies prior to their reuniting. As before, elevating the cardinal essences of the flower is conducted at a working stone enclosed in a protective circle of sea salt (see page 50 for instructions). In this working the practitioner will need to place upon the working stone all three bottles, each containing the cardinal essences of the dandelion; a ceramic bowl, preferably with a spout, to receive each essence as it is elevated; a clean linen cloth to clean and dry the bowl between each of the three elevations; and a suitable wand with which to elevate the essences. Here, as this potion is crafted as an empowerment potion, we will use a newly harvested standard Druidic living wand, harvested and potentialized as described earlier in the chapter (see page 70).

To begin the working, place the ceramic bowl at the center of the working stone and lay the energized wand across the top of the bowl. The small bottle containing the first of the cardinal essences is then held in both hands and raised high above the stone. Focusing upon the bottle, the practitioner says:

This essence has been extracted from the dandelion flower with all the care and knowledge inherited from my Druidic ancestors. I call upon the whole of nature to empower this essence and this working, as it has done since the beginning of time.

The bottle is then lowered, and its cork removed. The liquid is then gently poured over the wand so that it drips into the ceramic bowl below. As the liquid flows over the wand, it is energized by the wand itself as it also absorbs the personal energy of the practitioner previously invested within it. When all of the essence has been poured from the bottle, it is placed aside, and the liquid is allowed to drip from the wand for a few more moments. The wand is then removed from the top of the bowl. The elevated essence is carefully poured back into its original bottle, which is then resealed and placed aside until it is to be reunited in the next stage of the working. The empty ceramic bowl and the wand are then wiped clean and dried with the linen cloth.

This same process is repeated for the remaining two cardinal essences so that all three are elevated in the same way. The wand need not be reenergized for each essence as the personal energy invested within it is more than sufficient for the entire working. Once this is complete, all three cardinal essences have been elevated and stand ready to be reunited to form the final flower potion.

Reuniting the Cardinal Essences

The final stage in crafting the potion is the reuniting of the three individual cardinal essences to form the eventual empowering potion. This is typically done immediately following the elevation working described above, in which case the same working stone may be used as it remains within the sealed protective circle. To achieve this final crafting, the practitioner will need all three elevated cardinal essences, the same ceramic bowl (cleaned and dried), the practitioner's wand (already energized from the previous working), a small bottle to contain the finished potion bottle, and a dark cloth or pouch with which to wrap the potion to protect it from exposure to the light.

The working begins by once again placing the ceramic bowl at the front and center of the working stone. The cardinal essence from each small bottle is then poured into the bowl so that they mingle. It is important that the dandelion flower material of each essence remains in its bottle and that following the working each may be returned to the location where it was initially harvested and returned to the ground with a brief invocation of thanks. The combined cardinal essences are then slowly stirred with the wand as a reuniting invocation is spoken. This invocation typically may be:

> *By reuniting these cardinal essences, I bring together the spiritual energies of the dandelion and its virtues. May this potion bring to its caster the most potent empowerment and bonding.*

When the practitioner is confident that the potion is successfully coalesced, the wand is placed aside, and the reunited potion is carefully poured into the small bottle and tightly sealed. The sealed bottle is then wrapped in the dark cloth or placed in the pouch to protect it from sunlight until it is to be cast.

Remember, as this example is one of an empowerment intention, focused upon amplifying the potency of a subsequent intention (a curse removal) cast by a female Druid in a sex magic working, the potion and its accompanying intention are to be cast to the female Druid herself. This being the case, the potion and intention are most likely to be cast by the same practitioner that crafted it.

Casting the Potion

The casting of the potion along with the intention has to be achieved during the sex magic working, as it is that working that is to be empowered. In order for the potion and its accompanying intention to effectively bind itself to the recipient, two events must occur simultaneously: the potion must be cast upon the recipient person, the female Druid, and the casting intention must be spoken at the moment of casting.

This casting must, of course, take place *before* the recipient female Druid casts her subsequent intention of removing the curse from the elderly lady.

This casting working differs significantly from the examples we saw earlier, in that the casting of the potion is done not only with the aim of the potion coming into contact with the recipient directly, but also with the objective of empowering the work of the recipient herself during the final stages of a sex magic rite.

For the purpose of this example, the practitioner has chosen to conduct the empowerment working herself during the sex magic working. In this instance, it is assumed that a protective circle has already been cast for the sex magic working itself. Here, the practitioner will not need a working stone upon which to conduct the working, as the reunited potion will be cast directly upon the recipient's skin. The practitioner casting the potion will require the reunited potion, her living wand, and a clean linen cloth.

Before beginning the physical casting of the potion, the practitioner must focus her concentration upon the process of the working. In this instance this means visualizing a source where the empowering energy is residing within the universal energy. This empowering energy may be a ball of light, a cloud of a particular color, or any similar visualization that the practitioner may imagine. The reason for this is that although we know that empowerment energy resides universally within the world spirit, to attract this fortuitous energy it must be envisaged as a single source. The practitioner then continues to visualize the pending working by attaching to that energy source any form of capture. Typically this may be a tether to tie around it, a bottle in which it may be sealed, or a casket in which it may be secured. The captured energy is then visualized as undertaking a journey from its source to where it is to be bound, in this case, from its source to the spirit of the female Druid as the subject of the sex magic working. When the visualized captured energy arrives at its destination, it is bound securely so that its energy may percolate throughout the female Druid's spirit and physical body. This then represents the capturing, journeying, and binding of the empowerment energy to its desired new location and is, of course, the entire purpose of the working. The reason for this rehearsal is that, like all Druidic workings, it should not begin until the entire process and its outcome is completely understood and memorized. The practitioner may choose to repeat this visualization any number of times until she is confident that the entire working is firmly embedded in memory. Once the practitioner is prepared in this way, the practical elements of the working may begin.

To cast the empowerment intention, the practitioner first chooses the appropriate moment during the sex magic working, the point just prior to when the female Druid casts her own intention. The practitioner pours the reunited potion from its bottle onto the skin of the recipient and massages it into the skin as she speaks the invocation, which may be similar to:

> *I cast this potion to the spirit and body of this person*
> *in the knowledge that it will empower and increase*
> *the energy that they employ.*

In doing this, the practitioner visualizes the potion reaching the source of the recipient's energy in the same manner it had been visualized earlier. This intention may be spoken loudly, whispered quietly, or even simply repeated silently within the caster's mind.

Following this initial casting, the practitioner may choose to enhance the potential energy of the intention by dipping the living wand in the remaining potion and flicking the liquid potion over the recipient's body with her living wand as the sex magic working progresses. Here we see the living wand being used in the form of an aspergillum or aspergil, casting empowered liquid toward its recipient. While doing so, the practitioner declaims:

> *I draw to this place the energy I seek.*

This action is repeated for as long as the practitioner considers it to be productive. Once the practitioner is confident that the energy is present within the recipient, she may withdraw from the working in the knowledge that her efforts have significantly increased the potency of the sex magic working. At this point, the working is complete, and all that is left to do is return both the remaining potion and the used wand to their original harvest location and restore them to nature with a brief invocation of thanks.

The examples shown above illustrate some of the various ways in which Druidic flower magic may be employed to confront and remedy the difficulties encountered by everyone in their normal, everyday lives. Though the examples are not comprehensive, they represent a number of circumstances we may encounter and give an insight into how flower magic may benefit us all. The examples explored may be modified to address other situations, and the flower directory in chapter 10 will help in identifying the most suitable flowers and workings to tackle a wide range of circumstances.

REMEDIES AND WELL-BEING

It has long been known that the constituents within a flowering plant may be used as remedies for a wide range of ailments and that they may also contribute to our general well-being on a day-by-day basis. Most of the world's cultures regularly employ the various components of flowering plants as cures and antidotes to the many illnesses people encounter in their lives, and many make use of them as both physical and spiritual remedies. The Druidic lore of Wales is no exception.

ॐ Crafting a Well-Being Potion from a Ragwort Flower

In this example we shall explore the crafting of a well-being potion. As with all Druidic flower potions, before any crafting takes place, the practitioner must assure himself that his choice of potion is the correct one. Here, there are two components to be considered: the first being which flower is most suited for the desired task, and the second the most appropriate form of carrier in which it should be infused.

In this example, the intention is to raise the male recipient's feeling of well-being and lift him from his emotional and spiritual depression. The ragwort flower is well suited to this task owing to its virtues of raising the spirits, increasing feelings of optimism, increasing self-confidence, and generally improving the sense of well-being. The crafting is to be done using a potion powder, as this provides an excellent means of casting and binding the potion, along with the opportunity to examine another form of extracting a flower's cardinal essences. In Druidic lore, a powder carrier is often used for casting intentions, typically in a method known as Druid's breath.

Though this potion is crafted as a potion powder, it would be equally as effective crafted by any of the methods describe. The most important thing to bear in mind is that this potion is intended to work on the spiritual aspects of the recipient and not directly as a physical intervention. Therefore it is most beneficial if used in conjunction with medication designed to work on the physical aspects and should never be used as a substitute for mainstream medical interventions.

⫸ Ragwort, common (*Jacobaea vulgaris*)

Irish: *buachalán buí* (yellow boy)
Scottish: *cushag* (big stalk)
Welsh: *llysiau'r gingroen* (ragwort plant)
Flowers: June to November

Other common folklore names for ragwort include: common ragwort, ragweed, stinking willie, tansy ragwort, benweed, St. James-wort, staggerwort, dog standard, cankerwort, stammerwort, and stinking nanny, ninny, or willy. Many of these folk names reflect the plant's physical characteristics and the consequences of its use. In ancient Greece and Rome, ragwort was considered to be an aphrodisiac and was called *satyrion*.

Ragwort is a common wild plant and can be found growing on waysides and grasslands. It has closely grouped, flat-topped clusters of bright yellow flowers, each having between twelve and twenty-four individual florets (see plate 12). The leaves are pinnatifid with serrated, toothed edges. Ragwort leaves produce a useful green dye and the flowers a dye that can produce yellow, brown, and orange hues. Ragwort should be considered as poisonous and in the UK is listed under the Noxious Weeds Act 1936. It should not be ingested or handled by individuals with sensitive skin.

On the Isle of Arran, off the western coast of Scotland, a tradition holds that the first fairies journey from there to Ireland by each picking a ragwort plant and flying astride it to their destination.

Harvesting and Preparing the Powder and Flower

To craft this upraising potion from a ragwort flower, we shall be macerating the individual components of the plant in a powder carrier to create a powder potion. To do this we need to harvest the two main constituents, the mineral powder and the ragwort flower with its leaves.

It is best to gather the mineral powder first, as this can be done at any time before the crafting of the potion. In this example, the mineral used is chalk, gathered from the shore of Lough Leane (from the Irish *Loch Léin,* meaning "lake of learning"), County Kerry, in Killarney, Ireland. Chalk has been chosen in this instance because it is extremely porous, which makes it an excellent carrier for our flower potion. Chalk from Lough Leane is especially light in color, soft, and fine in texture and is simple to gather. The gathered chalk pieces are washed, dried, and ground to a very fine powder in a mortar and pestle. If the resulting powder appears to be gray in color or shows any unwanted adulterants, sieve it to remove the inclusions and, if necessary, wash the powder once again, spread it out to dry, and regrind it as done previously. This may be done repeatedly until the practitioner is happy that the chalk is clean and pure. It is imperative that the chalk is ground to the finest powder possible, even though this may take some time and effort to achieve. The chalk carrier may be stored indefinitely in a tightly sealed vessel and placed in a dry place until it is needed. With the fine chalk powder ground and stored, the appropriate time to harvest the ragwort is then planned. This must be as close as possible to the time it is to be crafted.

The first practical stage is the identification of an appropriate individual ragwort flower; this is done using the same criteria described previously. Once an individual flower has been identified, it is harvested by the same means and method described previously. However, in this example, because the potion and its accompanying intention is to be cast upon a male recipient, the flower and its leaves must be harvested in sunlight, ideally when the sun is at its highest. The harvested flower and leaves are then maintained in the same manner as detailed until it is to be crafted.

The first stage in the working is deconstructing the flower head and the leafstalk. The ragwort flower head is made up of two principal component parts, the petals and the flower head. The deconstruction methodology has been explained earlier under the dog rose potion and once completed leaves us with the individual flower petals, the flower head, and individual leaves (the same number as there are petals), all prepared for the next stage of the working (see plate 13).

Extracting the Cardinal Essences

The process of extracting the three cardinal essences from the three component parts of the ragwort is achieved in this example by means of powder maceration. For this particular working, the practitioner will need three small bowls (or, as shown, three small ceramic trays) and the storage vessel containing the ground chalk carrier, together with the three component parts of the ragwort that have previously been separated in the deconstruction working.

A layer of the powdered chalk is put into each of the three small trays, sufficient to make a bed upon which the flower parts are to be laid. The flower's petals are then placed on the bed of chalk in the first tray. The same is done with both the flower head and the leaves (see plate 14). Each flower component is then covered completely with the chalk powder (see plate 15).

The three small trays are then placed on a larger platter and covered with a sheet of clear glass to protect the precious powder from the wind and rain.

They are then placed in a location where they are directly exposed to sunlight and moonlight for a minimum of seven days to allow the powder to absorb the virtues of the ragwort flower. Following this, each of the three flower components' powders may be carefully poured into a separate bottle along with the flower components themselves. Each individual bottle is then tightly sealed.

Following this sun and moon energizing, the three cardinal essence powders are stored in a cool, dark place until they are to be used. It is important during this storage time that the component parts remain in the powder carrier. These cardinal essences may be stored in this way for up to six months. When the final potion is to be crafted, the three vessels containing the essences are retrieved so that they may be individually elevated as the next stage in the crafting.

Elevating the Cardinal Essences

Elevating the cardinal essences amplifies their physical and spiritual energies prior to their reuniting. As this is the first part of the potion crafting that involves the extracted cardinal essences of the flower, it must be conducted within a cleansed and protected environment. We must first construct a protective circle with a working stone located within it as we have done previously. The practitioner places upon the working stone the three bottles, each containing a separate cardinal essence powder of the ragwort as crafted above; a ceramic bowl, preferably with a spout, to receive each essence powder as it is elevated; a clean linen cloth to clean and dry the bowl between each of the three elevations; and a suitable wand with which to elevate the essences. As this potion is crafted as an upraising potion, we will use a newly harvested standard Druidic living wand, harvested and potentialized as described earlier in this chapter.

To begin the working, place the ceramic bowl at the center of the working stone and lay the energized wand across the top of the bowl. The small bottle containing the first of the cardinal essence powder is then held in both hands and raised high above the stone. Focusing upon the bottle, the practitioner says:

> *This essence has been extracted from the ragwort flower with all the care and knowledge inherited from my Druidic ancestors. I call upon the whole of nature to empower this essence and this working, as it has done since the beginning of time.*

The bottle is then lowered, and its cork removed. The powder is then gently poured over the wand so that it falls into the ceramic bowl below. As the powder flows over the wand, it is energized by the wand itself, and it also absorbs the personal energy of the practitioner previously invested within it. When all of the essence powder has been poured from the bottle, it is placed aside. The wand is then removed from the top of the bowl. The elevated essence powder is carefully poured back into its original bottle, which is then resealed and set aside until it is to be reunited in the next stage of the working. The empty ceramic bowl and the wand are then wiped clean with the linen cloth, ready for the next elevation.

This same process is repeated for the remaining two cardinal essence powders so that all three are elevated in the same way. The wand need not be reenergized for each essence as the personal energy invested within it is more than sufficient for the entire working. Once this is complete, all three cardinal essences have been elevated and stand ready to be reunited to form the final flower potion.

Reuniting the Cardinal Essences

The final stage in crafting the potion is the reuniting of the three individual cardinal essences to form the eventual upraising potion. This is typically done immediately following the elevation working described above. This being the case, the same working stone may be used as it remains within the sealed protective circle. To achieve this final crafting, the practitioner will need all three elevated cardinal essences, the same ceramic bowl (cleaned and dried), the practitioner's wand (already energized from the previous working), and a small casket or box to contain the finished potion.

The working begins by once again placing the ceramic bowl at the front and center of the working stone. The cardinal essence from each small bottle is then poured into the bowl so that they mingle. It is important that the ragwort flower material of each essence remains in its bottle and that following the working each may be returned to the location where it was initially harvested and returned to the ground with a brief invocation of thanks. The combined cardinal essences are then slowly stirred with the wand as a reuniting invocation is spoken. This invocation may be:

> *By reuniting these cardinal essences, I bring together*
> *the spiritual energies of the ragwort and its virtues.*
> *May this potion bring to its caster the most potent*
> *upraising and bonding, lifting from them all*
> *unnecessary concerns and worries and restoring to*
> *them an all-embracing sense of well-being.*

When the practitioner is confident that the potion is successfully coalesced, the wand is placed aside, and the reunited potion is carefully poured into the small casket or box and tightly sealed so that it will be protected from sunlight until it is to be cast. In this instance, the potion powder is to be cast by the same practitioner who crafted it, by a method known as the Druid's breath.

Casting with the Druid's Breath

The casting of powder potions may be done in a number of ways, including simply pouring the potion powder onto the recipient as the intention is recited or placing a deposit of the powder in a place where the recipient will come into contact with it as the practitioner recites the invocation. On this occasion, however, we will explore the casting method known as the Druid's breath. In this casting the practitioner blows or breaths the powder potion onto the recipient's body so that it makes contact with his skin and thereby binds the cast intention to the recipient. This in turn may be done in a number of ways, the most common being to place a measure of the potion powder on the outstretched palm of the hand and then blowing it onto the recipient, but in this example, we will use a magpie feather, much admired for its binding attributes, to hold the powder and cast it. As the practitioner must cast the potion powder directly onto the skin of the recipient, she must be close enough to him to ensure that this is possible. The practitioner casting the potion will require the reunited potion powder and a flight feather from a magpie bird (see plate 16).

Before beginning the physical casting of the potion, the practitioner must focus her concentration upon the process of the working. In this instance, this means visualizing a source where the upraising energy is residing within the universal energy. This upraising energy may be a ball of light, a cloud of a particular color, or any similar visualization that the practitioner may imagine. The reason for this is that although we know that upraising energy resides universally within the world spirit, to attract this fortuitous energy it must be a single source. The practitioner then continues to visualize the pending working by attaching to that energy source any form of capture. Typically this may be a tether to tie around it, a bottle in which it may be sealed, a casket in which it may be secured, or so on. The captured energy is then visualized as undertaking its journey from its source to where it is to be bound, in this case, to the spirit of the recipient. When the visualized captured energy arrives at its destination, it is bound securely to it so that its energy may percolate throughout the recipient's spirit and physical body. This then represents the capturing, journeying, and binding of the upraising energy to its desired new location and is, of course, the entire purpose of the working. The reason for this rehearsal is that, like all Druidic workings, it should not begin until the entire process and its outcome is completely understood and memorized. The practitioner may choose to repeat this visualization any number of times, certainly until she is confident that the entire working is firmly embedded in the memory. Once the practitioner is prepared in this way, the practical elements of the working may begin.

For this, the practitioner positions herself close enough to the recipient for the potion powder to reach its goal. Holding the magpie feather in the right hand, a measure of the potion powder is poured onto the feather tip. The practitioner then blows the powder toward the recipient. As it travels to its goal, the practitioner speaks the following invocation or something similar:

> *I cast this potion in the knowledge that it will bring*
> *to its recipient a settled mind, greater well-being, and*

a feeling of universal contentment. I do this in the tradition of my forebears and the great Druids of the past and present, in the certainty that these virtues will bind themselves and mingle with the personal energy of their recipient.

When this invocation is completed, a second casting of the potion powder is delivered by the same Druid's breath process. Once the practitioner is confident that the energy of the potion is present within the recipient, she may withdraw from the working in the knowledge that her efforts have significantly improved the spirit and mind of the recipient. At this point, the working is complete, and all that is left to do is return both the remaining powder potion and the used magpie feather to their original harvest location and restore them to nature with a brief invocation of thanks.

We have seen above how Druidic flower magic potions can be used effectively in a wide variety of circumstances and how they may be crafted and cast in an equally varied number of ways. Though the examples above do not cover every eventuality, they demonstrate how similar techniques may be adapted in almost unlimited permutations to suit the practitioner's requirements, and that a creative practitioner may modify the examples in new and never before seen ways to address any circumstance he may encounter in the modern world. Druidic flower magic is a living tradition, using living materials and spirits to achieve its beneficial results. It must be employed with wisdom and skill, using the accumulated knowledge of the past to tackle the difficulties of today and to improve all our combined futures.

SEVEN

Stocking the
Flower Magic Pantry

Having explored the many ways in which Druidic flower magic potions may be used and the various methods of crafting and casting potions created from the three cardinal essences extracted from each single flower, we will now look at the other ways that flowers are used to best effect in Druidic lore. While flower potions are extremely versatile and may be used in a large variety of circumstances, their potency comes directly from the extraction of the flower's attributes and virtues by macerating the relevant parts of the flower in a solvent or carrier. It is also possible to utilize other assets of flowers by employing the whole or part of it in Druidic ritual, where its benefits add potency and can contribute significantly to the intended outcome. In many such instances, the flower may be used for its fragrance, as a magic device, or even as a means of captivating a spirit or energy. In a similar way, flowers may be used as protective devices, preoccupying witches with ill intent or confusing their familiars and deterring them from their work. In the examples that follow, we shall be exploring the construction of a flower pouch to be used as a love attraction and binding device and the use of thorns from a blood-thorn briar in crafting a draught used as an apotropaic device, which protects against curses and malevolent energies.

FLOWER POUCHES

As with all potions and workings, the first stage in crafting a flower pouch is deciding if it is the most appropriate way to achieve the desired result. Flower pouches are most often used when there is a need for a complex intervention, as they are usually crafted from a combination of various flowers; each flower has its own virtues, and when merged with others the result may be enhanced or adjusted by the combination of the flowers' virtues. These combined flower pouches work in a similar way to complex potions, which are crafted from more than one flower. An important aspect of flower pouches is that they are crafted from whole, fresh flowers, unlike flower magic potions where the flower is deconstructed. Flower pouches may also contain other botanicals, animal components, and minerals, which make them more versatile than simple flower potions, allowing them to be used for circumstances where ordinary flower potions may not be as effective.

✿ Crafting a Flower Pouch from Thyme, Lavender, Mint, and Forget-Me-Not Flowers

This flower pouch is crafted using a combination of thyme, lavender, mint, and forget-me-not flowers. We shall also see how this same pouch may be enhanced by adding other components like bone and feathers. This is an example of a powerful love-enhancing flower pouch that would be employed in a situation where other attempts to attract a binding, lasting love between two individuals have not been effective. The working will involve four potent, love-attracting flowering plants that, when combined, produce a powerful and lasting love flower pouch. First we will look at the virtues of the individual plants that we have chosen to use.

⟿ Thyme, common (*Thymus vulgaris*)

Irish: *tím chreige* (rock thyme)
Scottish: *tìom* (thyme)
Welsh: *teim* (thyme)
Flowers: March to September

The extraordinary properties of thyme have been used by mediciners and cunning folk for millennia. The ancient Egyptians included it as part of their embalming formula, and the Greeks used it both to purify their baths and as a temple incense believed to imbue courage. During the Crusades, thyme became known as "the knight's herb," as wives would give their husbands small bouquets of thyme as they left on their mission as a token of courage and of their enduring love. This may well have been inherited from more ancient traditions where warriors would tie bunches of thyme to their thighs or stuff their shoes with the herb as a symbol of courage. Thyme is also associated with fairies who may bring good health and prosperity. In this instance, we are including thyme in our love pouch to employ its virtues of lasting love and emotional courage.

ᨃ Forget-me-not, field (*Myosotis arvensis*)

Irish: *lus míonla goirt* (salty herb)
Scottish: *dìochuimhnich-mi-chan* (no translation)
Welsh: *ysgorpionllys y meusydd* (unhappy partner)
Flowers: April to October

Other common names include: bird's eye, robin's eye, mammy-flower, snake-grass, love-me, scorpion grass, mouse ear. The name first appeared in French where it translated as *ne m'oubliez pas.*

The forget-me-not's small blue flower was used by the Freemason Grand Lodge Zur Sonne (The Sun) in 1926 as a Masonic emblem. This enabled Freemasons to wear the forget-me-not badge as a secret sign of membership. The forget-me-not is used in a large number of flower magic traditions for its virtues of attracting true love and sincere ties of love, and it is these virtues that we are employing in this example.

ᨃ Lavender, western sea (*Limonium recurvum*)

Irish: *lus liath na Boirne* (Burren gray herb)
Welsh: *lafant* (lavender)
Flowers: July to August

This small, delicate wildflower grows on the western seaboard of Ireland in a region known as the Burren. It is a low-growing plant, impervious to the salt-laden winds arriving from the western Atlantic. This perennial plant, native to West Ireland, is ideally suited to this application. Western sea lavender shares some of its attributes with the more common forms of lavender (*Lavendula*) and is used here for its virtues of love, binding, and physical relaxation. Lavender is used in many forms of flower magic, folk magic, and green witchcraft.

⇶ Mint, corn (*Mentha arvensis*)
Irish: *mismin arbhair* (corn mint)
Scottish: *mint arbhair* (corn mint)
Welsh: *mintys yr ŷd* (corn mint)
Flowers: August to September

Corn mint is native to Ireland and shares many of its attributes with the more common forms of mint found elsewhere. The many variants of mint are typically used by most schools of magic for their virtues of attracting love, wealth, and feelings of well-being. It is also used as a protection against evil, nightmares, and the evil spirits of darkness, and many esoteric practitioners use mint as an aid to divination. In this instance, we are using corn mint for its virtues of attracting love, its energy of renewal and emotional courage, and its attribute of protecting from unwanted, malevolent energies.

Harvesting, Elevating, and Casting the Flowers

Each of these flowering plants is harvested employing the same criteria as described earlier, giving due consideration to both the recipient(s) and the way in which the flowers are to be used. In this instance, the four botanicals are elevated together as a means of increasing their potential and amplifying their energies. This is achieved through an elevation working similar to those we have seen previously.

The plants are initially placed on a working stone within a cast, sealed, and cleansed protective circle, along with the small fabric pouch that will hold them (see plate 17). Then the practitioner, facing north, raises the bouquet of all four botanicals high into the air and speaks an invocation that may be similar to:

I call upon the eternal universal spirit to imbue these
gifts with its potent energies in the same way as it
has done for our forefathers and foremothers since
the beginning of time.

Turning to face east, the invocation is repeated, as it is again in the direction of the south and the west. The elevated botanicals are then placed within the pouch where they are secured in preparation for their casting. Casting the pouch may be as simple as placing it beneath the recipient's pillow, placing it in the recipient's pocket, or even secretly sewing it within the recipient's clothing, the important aspect being that it should be in as close contact with the recipient as possible.

THE BLOOD-THORN BRIAR AND PROTECTION

Not all flower magic potions are used in such a positive way, and some of the other products of flowering plants may be used in much more dramatic circumstances. A particularly potent example of this is the use of the thorns of a striking briar as a means of protection from malevolent energy.

The blood-thorn briar is an uncommon flowering briar that, during its mature cycle, displays spectacular blood-red thorns on light green branches, making it a valuable resource for all practitioners of Druidic flower magic. The briar will normally produce white or pink flowers during the blooming season, which themselves are used in other potions and philters, but it is the plant's bright-red thorns that we shall focus on here.

Thorns, by their very nature, are protective: their sole purpose is to protect the plant, its fruits and flowers, from damage by grazing animals. Spiky, sharp, and often hooked, thorns have evolved to safeguard whichever species they adorn. It is not difficult, therefore, to understand why they have been used for workings related to physical and spiritual protection since the beginning of the Druidic tradition.

Branches of briar thorns have been placed above thresholds, windows, fireplaces, and other vulnerable places around homes and farm buildings since medieval times to prevent the entry of unwanted malevolent spirits and witches and their familiars. In this example, a potion is to be crafted for a recipient who is concerned about the presence of an unwanted spirit energy.

✎ Crafting a Blood-Thorn Briar Protection Potion

Individual thorns may be removed from a briar's branch without having to cut the entire branch from the briar. Each thorn is carefully removed from the branch at spaced intervals, leaving at least ten thorns between each one that is removed. In this way the plant has the ability to heal the wounds on the branch resulting from the harvesting and can continue to thrive. A total of five thorns are harvested, though three is sufficient if the plant is small; bear in mind that each thorn has its individual energy extracted by individual maceration, so if a single potion is required, only a single thorn need be harvested. The thorns are selected and harvested employing the same criteria as we have seen previously and then kept in a sealed jar until the potion working takes place.

As with the other examples we have seen, this potion's crafting is achieved by a process of maceration to extract its protective properties. In this instance, however, the simple thorn cannot be deconstructed in the same way as the flowers that we looked at earlier; instead, the single thorn will be immersed in fermented mead for maceration and then the potion will be elevated by ritual and cast by being given to the recipient to drink. Although it may be argued that this method is less potent than the extraction, elevation, and reuniting of the cardinal essences that we saw with previous flower magic potions, this is compensated for by two singular aspects: the first being that the energy and strength of the thorn is much more evident than the delicate virtues of the flower, and second that, as the potion is to be drunk by the recipient, it is absorbed into the body and spirit in a more direct and efficient way.

Once more, the working takes place on a working stone within a cast, cleansed, and sealed protective circle. The working stone is prepared by placing the blood-thorn, mead, and a small bottle to hold the potion at its center. A single thorn is placed into the small bottle and covered with mead (plate 9). The bottle is sealed and placed in a position where it is exposed to sunshine during daylight and moonlight at night so that both energies will enhance the absorption of the thorn's protective energies.

It remains in this position for at least five days, after which it is stored in a cool, dark place until it is to be elevated and cast. These types of workings are often undertaken along with other workings to take full advantage of the cast protective circle.

When the potion is to be cast and the recipient is present, the mead potion is poured into another small bottle while the thorn is held back in the original bottle.

Note: It is very important that the thorn is removed from the potion before it is given to the recipient to drink as it may cause serious injury if it enters the recipient's mouth or if it is swallowed.

Before passing the potion to the recipient, the practitioner raises it high and recites an invocation that may be similar to:

> *This potion had been crafted from the blood-thorn*
> *briar to offer its protective energies to one who*
> *desires it. May it protect from every unwanted*
> *malevolent energy that may seek to enter the body*
> *and spirit, driving away all harmful influences*
> *and intentions.*

Having elevated the potion in this way, it is then given to the recipient to drink. This completes the crafting, elevation, and casting of the potion, and all that remains is to return the thorn to the location of the plant from which it was harvested, where it is returned to the ground with a brief invocation of thanks.

SIMPLES AND COMPLEXES

All flower magic potions are one of two types: a simple or a complex. A simple is a potion made entirely from one flower. As we have seen previously, these simple potions are crafted by extracting each of a specific flower's cardinal essences separately, elevating them to amplify their virtues, and finally reuniting them to create the finished potion, which is then used or cast to induce its precise and targeted effect. Potions crafted as simples are critically focused to achieve a very potent and directed result.

A complex is created by combining any number of simples. Each simple is crafted individually and then combined to produce the desired effect. In this way the individual virtues and attributes of any number of flowers can be coalesced to create a subtler influence or a wider acting effect where more than a single virtue is necessary. Such complexes are crafted for a very specific purpose where the individual properties of flower potions are combined, not only to address multifaceted circumstances but also to complement, enhance, and empower each individual virtue.

✢ Crafting a Complex of Dog Rose and Forget-Me-Not Potions

In the following example, a love philter is combined with a binding potion. We will use a love philter crafted from a dog rose (*Rosa canina*) as we have seen above and a binding potion crafted from a field forget-me-not (*Myosotis arvensis*) fashioned in the same way. The focus here will be on the commingling of the potions rather than the crafting of the individual potions. This particular potion is intended to be a powerfully binding love philter cast upon a male recipient, and as such it uses a well-established love philter with its binding energies enhanced and amplified by fusing it with a second potion that has potent binding properties.

The coalescing working takes place at a working stone within a cast, cleansed, and sealed protective circle. The small potion bottles containing the reunited cardinal essences of the dog rose and the forget-me-not, along with a ceramic bowl in which the potions are to be combined, are placed at the center of the working stone. In addition to these, a small bottle to contain the combined potion and the practitioner's living wand are laid on the working stone (see plate 18).

The working begins as the practitioner raises the dog rose philter high and speaks an invocation that may be similar to:

This philter, in all its potency, is to be a component in a complex along with other potions selected to complement and enhance its energies. I call upon the universal energy of nature to promote its honest use and instill within it and its accompanying potions the essential energies, as has been done by our ancestors in the past and will be done by our successors in the future.

The potion bottle is then lowered and unsealed and its contents poured into the ceramic bowl prepared to receive it. This is then repeated for the forget-me-not potion in exactly the same manner. The practitioner then stirs the combined potions with the living wand, reciting:

Let these potions mingle and coalesce, let their energies, virtues, and attributes fuse and complement each other and their combined purpose be fulfilled with only good intent.

The complex, as it may now be called, is poured carefully into the bottle prepared to receive it, which is sealed and placed in a dark cloth pouch until the potion is cast.

The potion is cast by bringing the liquid into contact with the recipient as the following incantation is spoken simultaneously.

May this potion fill [Name] with feelings of love and desire and may it unite him with [Name] and bind their union and spirits for all time in life and thereafter.

With this, the working is complete, and all that remains is for any remaining potion(s) to be returned to nature by pouring them onto the ground with a brief thanksgiving.

෨

The pouch and potions described above are just a few examples of the many ways flower magic may be used to address almost every conceivable circumstance by one means or another. These combined potions and pouches can be created using all the components that nature provides, either in their fresh, natural form or by crafting them through well-established Druidic workings accessible to all practitioners and their apprentices. We have seen that all these workings depend entirely on newly harvested botanicals and are completely dependent on the provenance of the components used with regard to their selection, harvesting, maintenance, crafting, and casting in order to achieve the intended outcomes.

There is, however, a range of commodities used in this form of flower magic that may be crafted from fresh, seasonal botanical materials at the time when they are plentiful and carefully stored until they are to be used. For the greater part, these commodities are used as carriers and other benign ingredients and each will always be subordinate to the freshy harvested flowers that define the practice of Druidic flower magic. This being the case, it is important that we look in some detail at these stored components as they play an indispensable role in the crafting of a wide range of simples and complexes.

A CUPBOARD OF POTIONS

The successful crafting of Druidic flower magic devices (be they potions, philters, pouches, or others, whether simples or complexes) frequently require additional components to augment the freshly harvested botanicals that form their core. As we have seen in our examples, these may be carriers, solvents, powders, or other components that are essential parts of the crafting and casting of any flower magic potion. Some of these commodities are seasonal and therefore must be gathered when they are at their best; others are gathered when most convenient as they may be stored without degrading, such as powders and spring water. Others need to be separately crafted over long periods of time, such as fermented mead and the like. Every practitioner will know that these types of commodities are essential and must be available whenever they are needed, so they are gathered, crafted, and stored in what may be called a cupboard of potions, even though such cupboards contain only the components and not the actual potions they make up. So that the reader may begin to accumulate these precious commodities in advance of their use, we shall look in some detail at what materials are essential, when they may be gathered and crafted, and how they may be stored to ensure their longevity and integrity.

Powder Carriers

The first essential materials we shall look at are carriers. For the greater part, carriers are benign materials, selected for their suitability in the extraction working where they are used to extract a flower's cardinal essences through a process of maceration. They are usually either powders or liquids; the liquids are either unadulterated and used in their natural state to craft a gentle, subtle potion, or they are fermented in a variety of ways to create a more powerful, vigorous carrier.

The practitioner's cupboard should contain a variety of powder carriers in order that the most appropriate for each circumstance may be selected. These should include (among others) chalk powder, grain flours, pollen, sea salt, and other ground mineral powders. All should be ground *very* finely, carefully dried, and stored in air-tight jars. Fine grinding and dryness are essential, as casting with powder is frequently enacted by the Druid's breath or feather methods described previously. It is always useful to accumulate as wide a range of powder carriers as are available as this gives the practitioner the broadest choice possible when it comes to crafting her potions.

Liquid Carriers

Liquid carriers may be divided into two main categories. The first consist of liquid solvents that are used in their natural state, such as spring water, rainwater, and honey. The second is made up of liquid solvents that need to be crafted and include such carriers as ales and meads (long and short versions), including the aforementioned metheglyn, a type of medicinal short-mead, and rhodomel, another short-mead fermented with rose hips that is used in many Druidic workings and rituals. Other short-meads are infused with blackberries, blueberries, whimberries (also known as billberries and whortleberries), raspberries, rowanberries, or whitethorn haws, each having its own characteristics and properties.

Water and Oil Carriers

The simplest form of carrier is pure spring water, but once again, the priority is the provenance of the supply. Store-bought spring water is not suitable no matter what claims of purity and wholesomeness the manufacturers may claim. The purity of the water is, of course, very important, but in this case, the source of the water is equally significant. The source should be directly from nature, as close to its emergence as practically possible. Ideally the spring water should be collected from a spring source and stored in a clean glass bottle in a dark place, preferably the potion cupboard, until it is needed. In some instances, fresh seawater may also serve the purpose as an effective carrier. In this case the salinity of the water must be taken into account when considering its influence upon the final potion. Bearing in mind that neither of these will be ingested, the spiritual purity of the water is equally important, if not more important, as its physical purity. However, if the practitioner is in any doubt, he should get the source checked with a laboratory sampling. Rainwater may be collected as another simple carrier, where the source is unadulterated either physically or spiritually. Rainwater collected during a thunderstorm (thunder water) is imbued with particularly powerful energies, as is rainwater collected during a lightning storm (lightning water).

As we have seen above, some workings require other simple liquids such as oil, and once again it is the provenance of these oils that is of greatest importance. The most frequently used forms of oils in Druidic workings are walnut oil and hazelnut oil, and both need to be pressed or removed by boiling from nuts harvested by the practitioner and not from store-bought nuts. Other, less frequently used carriers include milk, butter and other fats, and, in cases of curse workings, urine.

Fermented Carriers

In addition to these simple carriers, many workings require the use of more complex carriers, the most popular of these being fermented carriers. While the reader may find a wide collection of recipes for the crafting of wines and ales from a variety of sources, here we will focus on the crafting of mead-based carriers as they provide the basis for so many variations using a single, simple process of crafting.

Mead may well be the oldest alcoholic beverage known to humankind. It is unique in that it is crafted from honey, which in itself has its own spiritual characteristics and properties. This ancient beverage is made by fermenting honey with water, and in most of the examples we shall be looking at, we will be augmenting it with botanicals with their own, carefully selected attributes and virtues. The defining characteristic of mead, however, is that the main source of the fermentable sugar that is converted to alcohol comes from honey.

It may be easy to taste the difference between honey from bees that have habitually fed on lavender flowers and those that have eaten heather blooms, but we need to refer to the ancient Druidic lore to determine the influence that their different feeding habits have on the spiritual energies of the honey they produce. This being the case, it is necessary to determine which flower the bees producing your honey have been feeding on and refer to the flower directory at the end of the book to consider what influence this may have on the spiritual balance of the mead you intend to craft. First then, we shall look at the crafting of a basic mead, an essential commodity in every potion cupboard.

๛ Crafting Basic Mead

As this mead is not intended to be the simple beverage that may be bought in stores all over the world, it is only crafted in small quantities, and because of this the method differs from that used in making larger commercial batches. As such, the liquid is not fermented in large demijohns but is allowed to ferment in small glass or earthenware flasks covered with a linen filter to prevent any airborne impurities entering the brew. As this working has not evolved as a scientific process, the method of crafting remains simple and the equipment required very basic.

Equipment Needed

- Small, thick-bottom saucepan for dissolving the honey-water mix by gentle heating.
- Funnel to aid in pouring the hot liquid into the fermentation flask.
- Small flask for fermentation; this may be glass, ceramic, earthenware, or any nonmetallic impervious vessel.
- Clean linen cloth and string to cover the opening of the flask, preventing any unwanted airborne impurities from entering the flask.
- Short length of tubing (optional) to siphon the clear mead off the yeast sediment; alternatively, the fermented liquid may be carefully poured from the flask, leaving any sediment behind.
- Large wooden spoon for stirring the hot honey-water solution.
- Druidic brewing wand; more about this below.

This method of crafting is used primarily for small quantities, and here we shall be describing the crafting of one-half liter (one U.S. liquid pint) of finished mead.

Ingredients

75 grams (2.5 oz.) honey from a known organic source, not store bought
One-half liter (one U.S. liquid pint) spring water
One teaspoon brewer's yeast
One-half teaspoon lemon juice

Method

Step 1: Sterilizing

As with all fermentation, it's important to have a clean, sterile environment so the yeast grows but not any other unwanted bacteria.

Before beginning, wash down your work space with warm soapy water before sanitizing all the equipment immediately before it is used.

This is done by following the instructions given with the chosen sterilizing medium. Ensure all the equipment is sterile, rinsed, and dried before the crafting begins.

Step 2: Crafting the Mead

Pour the 75 grams of honey into the saucepan and add one-half liter of spring water. Bring to a gentle simmer, stirring all the time. Allow to simmer for no more than one minute, and then place saucepan aside to allow the liquid to cool.

In a separate cup, place three teaspoons of tepid (blood temperature) spring water. Sprinkle the brewer's yeast into the spring water and stir to dissolve. Once the yeast has dissolved, add the lemon juice to the same cup and leave for at least twenty minutes to proof.

Once the honey solution has cooled to room temperature, add the yeast solution and stir vigorously. This is called pitching the yeast. Now stir again using the brewing wand to invigorate the fermentation.

Pour the mixture into the fermentation flask. Fold the piece of linen to form at least four layers, and place over the flask opening and secure with string to form a filter.

Place the flask aside in a warm place to allow the initial fermentation to begin. This initial fermentation will begin after approximately six hours when it becomes very vigorous, and it may be helpful to place the flask on a deep dish to catch any overflow from the fermentation. If the liquid effervesces to the point where it soaks the linen filter, remove the linen and wash it thoroughly before replacing it.

After two days, the energetic fermentation will subside. This heralds the next stage of fermentation where the brew must be deprived of oxygen. This is done by removing the linen filter and replacing it with an airlock or loose stopper. The flask is then stored in a warm dark place where it won't be disturbed for two to three weeks. The fermentation may take longer, depending upon the conditions, such as temperature and humidity. When the fermentation is complete, the bubbling will stop, and you will see a layer of sediment formed at the bottom of the flask. This is the dead yeast and is completely natural. At this point, place the flask in a refrigerator for one or two days, which will cause the yeast to become dormant and aid in clearing the mead.

After the mead becomes clear, the mead must be separated from the dead yeast or it will contaminate the mead. This is done either by siphoning the clear liquid off the sediment into a second sterile flask or very carefully pouring the clear liquid from the flask while leaving the sediment behind. Carefully clean and sterilize your original flask, transfer your mead back into it, and seal the flask tightly.

Step 3: Conditioning the Mead

Let the flask stand at room temperature away from direct sunlight for two to six weeks to condition. The finished mead may then be safely stored in your potion cupboard until it is needed.

USING MEAD AS A CARRIER

Crafting mead is a relatively simple, age-old process, and it may be confusing to relate it to modern wine- or beer-making techniques, as it is a much more informal, natural process. The potency and energies of the ingredients may vary significantly from brew to brew, and the fermentation process will vary according to the season, temperature, and ability of the practitioner, so be prepared to persevere with your crafting, adapting the method and ingredients to best suit your personal conditions.

Mead, for the greater part, is a benign carrier. Even though we have seen that honey, its principal ingredient, does indeed have some attributes and that these attributes may have some effect upon the finished potion, they are benign influences as honey's main virtues are its gentleness and healing properties, which will always have a positive effect. One of the ways mead may be used in Druidic workings is as a carrier for other flower potions where it is used as a macerating solution as we have seen in chapters 6 and 7, in which case the mead is chosen to amplify the positive effects and/or healing attributes of the flower potion. In these instances, the selected flower is deconstructed and macerated as separate parts to extract the flower's three cardinal essences before they are eventually reunited to craft the final flower magic potion. When used in this way, the mead is used as a carrier; however, in other circumstances, the botanicals are added to the mead before fermentation, and chief among these flower fermented meads is metheglyn, the famous Druidic healing mead. Metheglyn is a Welsh portmanteau word: *methe*, referring to medicine and healing, and *glyn* being the Welsh word for "wine."

Metheglyn is a form of short-mead fermented with a variety of indigenous herbs (not flowers), the most common combination being wild thyme, sage, lovage, and mint. The herbs are bruised and added to the honey-water solution as it is heated; otherwise, the method of crafting is exactly the same as with simple mead. The herbs remain in the brew until the mead is separated from its sediment at which time the herbs remain in the flask along with the sediment. A more potent and psychotropic version of metheglyn is crafted using wormwood and yarrow.

In addition to these herb-infused metheglyns, a similar technique may be used incorporating flowers instead of herbs. Most popular among these is marigold mead, which is a modest potion used to increase wealth and prosperity. As with herb metheglyn, all flower mead potions are crafted by adding the whole of the selected flower and a proportionate number of leaves to the honey-water solution as it is heated and leaving them in the fermenting mead until it is drawn off, leaving behind the sediment and flower components, once the fermentation has finished. In this way all the energies and attributes of the marigold (or other flower) are absorbed by the mead. This is a subtler and more gentle way of crafting flower potions that produces a much milder form of potion and may be crafted from any individual flower as needs require.

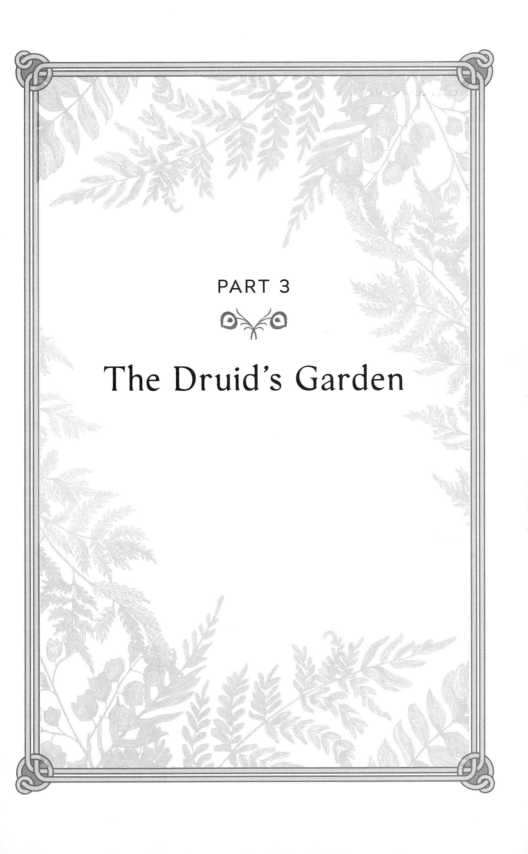

PART 3

The Druid's Garden

EIGHT

Bees, Flowers, and Druids
A Symbiotic Relationship

Ask the wild bee for what the Druid knew.

TRADITIONAL WELSH, SCOTTISH, IRISH SAYING

It is not possible to discuss the Druidic tradition of flower magic without including a section on bees. Not only are they regarded as the custodians of great arcane supernatural knowledge, but they are also considered as the messengers between the mundane world and the world of the other.

The British Isles have long benefited from a prolific population of bees, and today, there are over 250 species of bees surviving in the UK: 25 species of bumblebees and 224 species of solitary bees, but only 1 of honeybee. Unfortunately, there has been an overall decline in wild bees and honeybees over the past fifty years, a predicament we shall discuss in more detail later. For us, the most famous species is the western honey bee (*Apis mellifera*), which has been the focus of beekeeping, or apiculture, for tens of thousands of years. Archaeologists have discovered fascinating evidence of pottery used by our ancestors to store honeycomb at least nine thousand years ago. Research teams from a number of European institutions reporting in the scientific journal *Nature* have found the distinctive chemical signature of honeycomb or beeswax on pottery shards in Northern Europe and elsewhere, where over the millennia they have fulfilled a variety of technological, magical, and cultural functions. When the Celts first ventured onto the British Isles and Ireland, they called Britain the Isle of Honey, as a reflection of the impressive number of bees filling the air. It has been argued that the European Celts originally came to Britain specifically for the famous black bee and its honey.

Druids, bees, and flowers have formed an inseparable relationship since prehistory, bound by their interdependence and symbiotic interaction. Bees gather pollen, nectar, and propolis from wildflowers, each an indispensable commodity for the bees, their colony, and their nest. In doing so, the bee pollinates the flower, an essential part of the flower's life cycle, which, in many cases, can only be done by the bee. Druids interact, safeguard, and nurture both flowers and bees, respecting them as providers of nature's gifts, earth wisdom, well-being, and access to the otherworld. In Druidic lore, bees are believed to have secret knowledge and the ability to communicate between the mundane and the otherworld, while flowers hold the treasured cardinal essences that give us access to the arcane world of Druidic magic.

STRUCTURE AND COMMUNITY

It is extraordinary to think that each bee may visit more than two million flowers to gather enough nectar to make a single pound of honey, and a foraging bee may travel up to ten miles per day to gather pollen and nectar to bring to the colony. It is no wonder that bees are associated with hard work and diligence. They live in a precisely organized matriarchal society. In their natural habitat, most bees live in colonies within nests, though some may live in smaller communities and yet others are known to be solitary. Each colony is made up of a single fertile female—the queen—a large number of nonreproductive females called worker bees, and a smaller number of fertile male called drones. The inhabitants of a nest containing a single colony of such bees may number in the tens of thousands. It is only when they are farmed by humans that they are housed in what we originally called *skeps,* the small woven-straw inverted baskets that later developed into the more sophisticated hives we know so well today. The pollen and nectar the worker bees work so hard to gather are shared with the entire community and stored in different sections of the hive until they are needed. The scout worker bees relentlessly search for new sources of food then return to the hive to communicate the location and quantity of the flowers they have discovered to the others through a complex wiggle-dance performance.

The heart of each colony is the queen, and her health and survival are the main preoccupation of the hive. She constantly broadcasts information on her condition throughout the colony by releasing telltale pheromones that the entire community is able to interpret. If her condition deteriorates, the worker bees feed royal jelly to selected larvae, which develop into a number of new queen candidates. The first queen out of her cell finds and kills the others and then leaves with a portion of the colony to establish her own colony.

As well as the prolific honeybee, we also regularly encounter the much-loved bumblebee, the most common in Western Europe being the buff-tailed bumblebee (*Bombus terrestris*). Also known as the large earth bumblebee, this much-loved bumblebee typically lives in holes in the ground and fissures hidden deep within the hedgerow. Known as the most private of bees, their nests are often very difficult to find. This friendly little bee will only sting if actively provoked, and its gentle nature makes it a popular candidate for commercial greenhouse pollination. In the old English language, a bumblebee was known as a dumbledore; in Welsh it is called *cacwn,* and in Irish it is known by the wonderful name of *bumbóg*. All bees are closely associated with the feminine, primarily as a result of their matriarchal society. They are also associated with the virtues of love and forgiveness and, of course, vital energy and creativity.

BEES IN HISTORY

A great deal has been written over the years about the role of the bee in ancient civilizations and their association with revered leaders such as the Egyptian pharaohs, who carried the symbolic title of beekeeper and used the honeybee as their royal symbol. The biblical ruler King Solomon consulted with a bee before courting the love of the Queen of Sheba, and the legendary strongman Samson's encounter with the bees emerging from the dead carcass of a lion is well known to Christian followers. Beyond these Old Testament references, the mystic branch of Islam, known as Sufism, maintained a secret brotherhood called *Sarmoung,* meaning "*bee.*" Members of this clandestine brotherhood consider it their duty to gather the precious honey of sacred knowledge, preserving it for future generations to come.

In more recent times, we see the bee become the emblem of French industry and, as a result, the principal symbol of the French Revolution (1789–1799). When Napoleon Bonaparte was crowned emperor of France in 1804, he wore a robe embellished with three hundred gold bees. He saw the bee as a symbol of immortality and resurrection or regeneration. The bee symbol continued to be hugely important during Napoleon's reign and gave rise to his popular nickname *l'abeille,* meaning "the bee." This small insect was no stranger to Napoleon; since his childhood in Corsica, he would have been aware of the annual tax paid to the Romans by the Corsicans in beeswax, a valuable commodity worth around 250,000 USD in today's money. The bee became a popular emblem during Napoleon's rule, and more than sixty cities throughout France and Europe selected an officially approved heraldic shield that included three bees as part of its design. Less than a decade before his coronation, Napoleon made a name for himself as a military general during his 1798 invasion of Egypt, which at the time was known as the "land of the bee," where he undoubtedly encountered the huge monolithic statues named after the Minoans' word for bee: *sphex*—the origin of the Greek word *sphinx.*

There are many other instances of bees being associated with esoteric traditions. These include the Freemasons, where both the bee and the beehive are vital symbols of Masonic principles as may be seen repeatedly within the Encyclopaedia of Freemasonry,* where we find the instructions for new initiates to:

---

*See online source, Andrew Gough, "Part 3: Beegotten," in *The Bee,* 2008.

Go to the bee, and learn how diligent she is, and what a noble work she produces; whose labour kings and private men use for their health. She is desired and honoured by all, and, though weak in strength, yet since she values wisdom she prevails.

The encyclopedia further states:

The bee hive is an emblem of industry, and recommends the practice of that virtue of all created beings. . . . Thus was man formed for social and active life, the noblest part of the work of God; and he that will so demean himself, as not to be endeavouring to add to the common stock of knowledge and understanding, may be deemed a drone in the hive of nature, a useless member of society, and unworthy of our protection as masons.

We also see the symbolism of the bee and hive in the teachings of Pierre Plantard, the founder of the Priory of Sion, who himself was an avid beekeeper.

Other influential occult masters—such as the German philosopher and founder of the Illuminati Johann Adam Weishaupt (1748–1830) and the British occultist Aleister Crowley (1875–1947), a principal member of occult traditions such as the Golden Dawn and Ordo Templi Orientis (O.T.O.)—incorporated the bee and the beehive as symbols of industry and altruism. Crowley, in fact, became infamous for wearing an unusual beehive-inspired headdress as a trademark. Weishaupt originally planned to call his secret society, founded in 1776, the Order of the Bees, but as a result of pressure from his Freemason colleagues, the society was eventually named the Order of the Illuminati.

The bee has been such a popular emblem mainly because of its industry and the fact that it serves others before it serves itself, putting the survival of the colony before its own well-being. This is epitomized by the writing of St. John Chrysostom, the fourth-century archbishop of Constantinople. Chrysostom, a nickname, means "golden mouth," so-called because of his famed oratory skills. He famously observed that:

The bee is more honoured than other animals, not because she labours, but because she labours for others. Indeed, the bee works unceasingly for the common good of the hive and obeys without question what sometimes appears to be an inequitable hierarchy.

There are many other esoteric traditions that include the symbolism of the bee, and a little research will provide the reader with a comprehensive list that ranges far beyond the purview of this exploration. But for now we will return to the countries of the so-called Celtic homelands of Ireland, Scotland, and Wales.

BEES IN IRELAND

Since well before the arrival of the Celtic influence in Ireland, the country was known for its population of bees and its copious supply of honey—so much so that the keeping of bees became governed by its own set of laws dedicated solely to beekeepers and farmers. These bee laws were called Bech Bretha, meaning "Bee Judgments," and were part of a collection of laws that covered the entire country, called the Brehon Laws, which contained all the laws relating to agriculture and the ownership of land and within which the laws relating to beekeeping were the most voluminous and precise. The law outlines rules related to bee trespass on other farmer's lands, fines for bee stings and compensation for anyone who died from a bee sting. Fines included payments in honey, mead, and even the forfeit of complete hives and swarms.

As well as these legal enactments, Irish folklore includes many references to bees, explaining how bees, both kept and wild, must be treated as members of the family, with friendship and consideration. Failure to do so results in the bees ceasing to produce honey, deserting their hives or even dying. The bees must be told of any important events such as births, deaths, marriages and such, and when a death occurs in a family, once the bees have been told, the entrance to their hive must be turned away from the home and the hive covered with a black cloth and the bees must be given a share of the funeral food and drink to honor their role as messengers between the worlds of the living and the dead.

One of the oldest pagan goddesses, Brigid, has a close association with bees, who brought nectar from her apple orchard in the otherworld, following rivers of mead that flowed between the two worlds. Brigid is also very much connected to marriage, her name being the suggested root of the word *bride* and potentially the source of the custom of the honeymoon through the tradition of the married couple eating honey each day for a month (a moon cycle) following their marriage. The later Christian saint Gobnait, said to be the Christianized version of Brigid, retained the close relationship with bees, using them to protect her followers and guard them from cattle thieves as well as using their honey to miraculously heal her flock of the plague. Gobnait established one of the first ever women's communities in the west of Ireland and is often seen as a bridging figure between the original pagan tradition and the newly introduced Christian beliefs that arrived in Ireland during the late Roman period in Britain. She has the reputation of being one of three sisters who had power over elemental fire and was believed to be the triple fire goddess, Brigid, sharing the same feast day in early February, halfway between the winter solstice and the spring equinox, known as Saint Brigid's Day (Irish: *Lá Fhéile Brí;* Scottish: *Là Fhèill Brìghde*). Called Imbolc, it is one of the four traditional annual festivals, along with Bealtaine, Lughnasadh, and Samhain. At one of her shrines at Ballyvourney, County Cork, she is depicted standing on top of a beehive, surrounded by a swarm of bees.

BEES IN SCOTLAND

In ancient Scotland, bees were revered for their purpose in pollinating flowers and other crops, renewing the abundant fecundity of the world. Beekeepers were considered holders of a sacred charge, nurturing the bees and harvesting the honey they produced. The making of mead was undertaken as a sacred ritual, and its consumption was a sacred privilege. Throughout the mainland and Scotland's many islands, the people once spoke of the secret learning of the bees—the hardy honeybees were the possessors of a secret and profound knowledge, known only to them and the most learned Druids. As with the bees of Ireland, their Scottish relatives were considered to be messengers between the mundane and the preternatural, carrying this knowledge.

The products of the precious bees—honey and mead—were commonly used for magic and medicine, and the canny Scots crafted a healing potion from heather honey, whiskey, and thick cream as a remedy for a wide range of ailments and disorders. In the more remote rural areas of the highlands, the tradition of feeding small children milk and honey is derived from the ancient practice of feeding babies whose mothers did not produce milk a wholesome feed of warm hazelnut milk mixed with honey. In the Western Isles or Outer Hebrides, folklore tells of an old hermit who lived a solitary life in the dense forest among a colony of honeybees. He was able to identify each individual bee and gave each a name and called his bee family "the tiny musicians of the forest." He is said to have lived on a diet of strong honey wine mixed with hazelnut milk and herbs.

The Scottish Highlanders held that while a person slept their spirit left in the form of a bee and traveled this world and the other, gathering sacred knowledge in the same way as the bees gather nectar in the daylight, bringing it back to the sleeper before he or she awoke. As with other traditions, bees were considered to be members of the family and never offended. If they were slighted or snubbed, they would stop producing honey and leave the hive. Following this, the beekeeper was destined to die.

BEES IN WALES

The history of bees in Wales is said to have begun when Hen Wen (the Old White One), the mystical sow goddess of Dadweir Dallpenn, dropped three grains of wheat and three bees onto the ground in the Welsh county of Gwent, after which the wheat flourished and the bees produced honey in quantity and quality seen nowhere else in the land. Since then, bees have held a prominent position in the lore of the Welsh and their Druids. The lore of bees and their relationship with death is especially spoken of; if there was a death in the family, it was important that someone in the family told the bees. A black ribbon was then tied to a wooden wand, which was put in the hole at the top of the hive to protect the family against any further deaths.

In the late ninth century, Hywel Dda (ca. 880–948), the king of Deheubarth, Wales, wrote the famous Laws of Hywel Dda (Welsh: Cyfraith Hywel), the first set of laws defining the laws of inheritance, land ownership, social behavior, marriage and divorce, and religious acceptance for all of his subjects. Hywel Dda, or Howel the Good, was also known as Hywel ap Cadwell (Howel son of Cadwell). He eventually became the ruler of the majority of Wales, and in compiling his Laws of Hywel Dda began what has become known as the Code of Dyfed, where he describes how he brought together expert lawyers and priests from each *commote* or, in Welsh, *cwmwd*, which means "a division of land," in Wales in the White House in Dyfed (Welsh: Tŷ Gwyn ar Daf) in order to codify the Laws of Wales. In addition to the legal subjects mentioned above, the Laws of Hywel Dda also governed the keeping of bees, the production of mead, and the responsibilities of the mead maker. Even so, much of the rural population still adhered to the ancient folklore of their ancestors, and a wide range of traditions continued to be upheld for many centuries to come. Among these ancient folklore traditions, we find that:

- A swarm that settles on a dead branch foretells a death in the beekeeper's family.
- A swarm entering a house is considered unlucky and also foretells death.
- If a swarm enters a garden it is good luck, but bad luck if it later leaves.
- A bumblebee buzzing at the window is a sign of a coming visitor. If you kill the bee, the visitor will bring you bad news.
- If a single bee enters your house, it is a sign of good luck and wealth.
- If the bees hear you quarreling or swearing, they will leave, so you must always speak to them in a gentle manner.
- Bees do not tolerate the presence of a woman with loose morals, or indeed one who is menstruating.

Other Welsh folk customs include presenting a new bride with a bee skep as a wedding present and token of good luck and, similarly, a piece of wedding cake is placed at the entrance to the beehive after the ceremony for good luck. Finally, at a funeral it is still customary to leave a biscuit dipped in wine at the entrance to the hive for the bees to enjoy once the guests have departed.

Throughout Wales, bees have always been associated with witches and witchcraft, and many Welsh witches were said to have a bumblebee as their familiar, sending the insect on all sorts of missions, including the casting of spells and curses.

As in the other Celtic lands, Welsh people thought that when sleeping, in a trance, or at the moment of death, the spirit left the body in the form of a bee—a belief that has clear Druidic origins. All Welsh Druids were learned in the art of soul flight, journeying to the otherworld to seek knowledge from the spirits of their ancestors. In the same way, Welsh witches were known to ride their brooms or staves through the dark night by means of flying ointments crafted from honey, beeswax, and a collection of psychotropic indigenous herbs and tree barks. Their nighttime journeys to create havoc on their mystical wooden staves or "horses" became known as *hunllef,* the Welsh word for "nightmare."

ANCIENT BEEKEEPERS, DRUIDS, AND MONASTIC HEALERS

History tells us that beekeeping was one of the first examples of farming among humankind and that even before humans began nurturing their own bees they were well acquainted with the benefits of the products of the bee in the wild.

It is reasonable to assume that beekeeping evolved in a similar manner to the selective growing of the many plants they pollinate. Our ancestors on the British Isles made regular use of the wildflowers and herbs they found growing around them in the meadows and woodlands and certainly became aware of the botanicals that played the most important roles in their medicinal, culinary, and magic practices. Finding it more convenient than foraging on a regular basis, these wise-women and cunning folk easily transferred the most popular varieties they needed from the wild and into their own cottage gardens, establishing the first culinary and medicinal gardens adjacent to their homes. In the same way, we may assume that acknowledging the benefits of the honeybees, so numerous in their surroundings, they captured and encouraged their local bees to swarm as close as possible to their dwellings, eventually crafting skeps to house their own swarms to produce their honey and pollinate their cottage gardens. This became such an important feature of the community that, as we have already seen, the establishment and maintenance of such swarms became enshrined in the early laws of the land, and any who failed to adhere to the law received the most stringent punishment. So once again, as we have seen so many times, the beginning of a practice that was to extend right up to the present day may be traced back to the learning and experience of the cunning folk of the pre-Celtic population of Wales, Ireland, and Scotland.

As Christianity embraced the pagan Isles of Britain, a number of these learned cunning folk, often described as Druids and witches, adopted the new faith, bringing with them the wisdom and practices of the old ways, including their knowledge of flower magic, botanical healing, and the nurturing of bees. As a direct result, almost every monastery, convent, and Christian commune quickly established their own medicinal and healing garden and collection of beehives. It was with the produce of these physic gardens, as they came to be known, and the honey from their beehives that we see the role of the monastic brother as herbalist and healer develop and how in Northern Europe, so far from the wine-growing regions of the south, we see the same brothers (and sisters) gain a reputation as brewers and vintners with their gentle crafting (and drinking) of the meads, ales, and medicinal brews that used their bees' honey as their base. It is from this enthusiastic beekeeping of monks, priests, pastors, and nuns that we see the major development in beekeeping throughout the Middle Ages. In particular, we should be thankful to Pastor Lorenzo Langstroth for the invention of the Langstroth hive, which itself was developed into the familiar Warre hive that we know today by Abbé Emile Warré, a French priest and beekeeper. Importantly, we also see the development of a new, more resilient species by Brother Adam of Buckfast Abbey in Devon, England, who bred the famous Buckfast bee, a variant that remains very popular with beekeepers up to the present day.

While it may be easy to attribute these crucial developments to the industry and diligence of the monks concerned, we must not forget two important aspects that also contributed to their knowledge. The first is the origin of the lore that informed the use and development of these practices: we find that the cunning folk employed the same lore for millennia before the establishment of the Christian monasteries and convents. The second is the more subtle influence apparent from the recently converted pagans, who embraced the burgeoning Christian establishment. These converts brought with them their belief that the botanicals and honey of the British Isles were a source of spiritual and magic power—which the new faith cleverly appropriated as Christian workings and miracles.

We know that Druids, both past and present, are often enthusiastic beekeepers and continue to acknowledge the role of the bee in pollination and honey production, as well as the bees' spiritual virtues and the model community of the beehive. Since time immemorial, Druids have recognized the bees' importance within the complexity of nature and revered bees as an indispensable aspect of the Druidic worldview.

THE BEES' GIFTS

Honey

Many belief systems speak of honey as the nectar of the gods, of a land of milk and honey, and of rivers of honey and mead showing the way to the summer lands of blissful eternity. Most also consider honey a magic substance, using it extensively in healing and ritual. In ancient Ireland and Wales, the Druids spoke of a land beneath the water where our ancestors live and where rivers pour forth a stream of honey, and people still make honey cakes to leave outside their door at Bealtaine to please visitors from the otherworld.

Without doubt, honey has played a significant part in not only the magic and healing traditions of Ireland, Wales, Scotland, and ancient Britain, but it has also influenced the food and drinking habits of countless cultures around the world. In medieval Britain a mixture of animal fat and honey was used extensively as a condiment, and small bowls of honey were placed beside each dinner plate so that diners could dip their meat or fish into the sweet nectar before eating it. Throughout Northern Europe, honey remained the only source of sweetening until the Crusaders brought sugar back from their journeys to the Middle East in the eleventh century.

A drink combining milk and honey remains an important element in Druidic ritual, as are mead, metheglyn, and *bragget,* a potent drink made from spiced ale and honey. Early ales were brewed without the use of hops as they are not native to the Isles of Britain. Instead, ales were "bittered" with indigenous herbs that were often psychotropic, including wormwood, yarrow, and others. These bitter, hallucinogenic brews were frequently sweetened with honey to make bragget and other similar everyday drinks.

In much more recent times, Swiss psychiatrist and founder of analytical psychology Carl Gustav Jung (1875–1961) recognized the importance of honey, saying that:

in the honey, the "sweetness of earths," we can easily recognize the balsam of life that permeates all living, budding, and growing things. It expresses, psychologically, the joy of life and the life urge which overcome and eliminate everything dark and inhibiting. Where spring-like joy and expectation reign, spirit can embrace nature and nature, spirit.*

---

*C. G. Jung, *Collected Works of C. G. Jung,* vol. 14, *Mysterium Coniunctionis: An Inquiry into the Separation and Synthesis of Psychic Opposites in Alchemy,* 2nd ed., trans. R. F. C. Hull (Princeton, NJ: Princeton University Press, 1977), 490.

In Druidic lore, honey is one of the most important and frequently used gifts of nature. Whether as an ingredient in ritual drinks and potions, including the forementioned Druidic love philter, or in the crafting of curative balms, ointments, lotions, and draughts related to Druidic flower magic, honey provides essential sweetness, love, and well-being for both the mundane and spiritual aspects of all our lives.

Beeswax

As with the bees' honey, beeswax (Latin: *cera alba*), naturally produced by special glands in the abdomen of each worker honeybee, has been employed in Druidic flower magic lore for time immemorial. It has long been important that Druids, whether students or established, spend time observing the bee colony and learning from their behavior. The structure of the colony, the behavior of the bee community, and the produce they work so diligently to create are all to be critically observed and remembered in minute detail.

In the earlier days of bee husbandry, the cunning folk who tended the colony provided them with a skep as a convenient home, but being a simple construction made from plaited straw, each skep was destroyed at the beginning of autumn in order to harvest the precious honey and beeswax. The bees' produce was, and still is, treated with the utmost respect and revered in acknowledgment of the hard work and innate knowledge the bees have shown in crafting their precious gifts. Modern beehives are constructed in such a way that they may continue to be used year after year, season after season, so taking beeswax from a hive has become more of a moral argument as the bee colony is known to use the wax honeycomb structure over and over again, even reusing the small beeswax caps they remove from the top of each cell that gather on the floor of the hive. As a result, most Druidic beekeepers use a well-proven method of selectively harvesting beeswax from specific areas within the hive that the bees can easily replace, enabling a sustainable colony while still allowing a limited beeswax harvest.

Beeswax is employed in a wide variety of uses within the Druidic tradition, from simply sealing bottles and jars to the meticulous crafting of ointments, salves, and other curative potions. One of the more unusual applications of beeswax in Druidic lore is the crafting of poppets or wax dolls, waxen images of individuals used for the casting and long-term binding of spells and curses, originally used by Druids and rural cunning folk and later adapted by wisewomen in their witchcraft workings. Examples of these may be seen in the collections of many British museums including the National Museum of Wales in Cardiff, South Wales. Other uses include the use of flat beeswax writing tablets, inscribed with curses and other spells or intentions (curse tablets); the crafting of candles; the modeling of animals and birds used in the same way as the poppets mentioned above; and strengthening natural thread made from indigenous flax. When crafting ointments and salves, beeswax may be diluted with vegetable or nut oils to create a soft, smooth lotion or a firmer salve, both of which melt and become absorbed when in contact with warm skin.

THE HEXAGON

In addition to the bees' perfectly ordered matriarchal community structure, the ancient Druids also looked toward the ideal physical structure of the bees' honeycomb and in particular the hexagonal form of each of the honeycomb's individual cells. As a result, the hexagon has been a principal symbol and underlying pillar of Druidic lore for millennia.

As discussed in my previous book *Witches, Druids, and Sin Eaters,* the hexagon represents a number of very significant correspondences, in particular the association with the queendom of the bee being a representation of the cells of the honeycomb and its association with the culture of the bee. This is further confirmed when we look at the six converging points of the hexagon.

At each corner of the hexagon is a convergence point; these are the six points or stations of the hexagon and each represents a source of elemental energy. When the protective circle is closed during Druidic workings, a vessel containing the appropriate elemental energies is traditionally placed at each station; some or all of these may be used in the working.

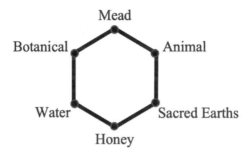

The six points (stations) of convergence.

The upper chevron of the hexagon represents the male phallus, the power and force of fertilization, and the upper half of the hexagon is the male domain. The lower chevron represents the cup or chalice of the female vagina and the womb of creation. The lower half of the hexagon is the female domain. The two supporting pillars are knowledge and wisdom, while the whole illustrates how the balance between male and female is maintained through the application of wisdom and knowledge.

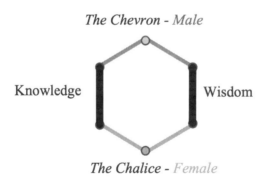

The male and female domains of the hexagon.

It is as a consequence of these pillars of knowledge and wisdom that Druidic lore has propagated the concept of conservation and respect for nature and her gifts. One of nature's most intelligent and industrious gifts is the bee, a precious gift that we are in danger of losing.

BEE PRESERVATION AND PROTECTION

We, as a global community, are responsible for the growing threat to the overall bee population, and we must accept that this critical environmental threat is not a new phenomenon. In the mid-twentieth century, Albert Einstein is reported to have said: "If the bee disappeared off the surface of the globe, then man would only have four years of life left." Whether this is correctly attributed to Einstein or not (and it is disputed by some), this quote clearly illustrates that such a result would be catastrophic for the planet and the civilizations that inhabit it and that the scientific community of the time was well aware of the magnitude of the threat.

We have long known that if plants are not pollinated, they will not set fruit or produce seeds. These plants include, of course, all our commercial and noncommercial food crops. In fact, over 70 percent of species that provide food worldwide are pollinated by bees, meaning that one out of every four bites of food you eat is thanks to the bee. It is also worth noting that the honeybee is the only insect that produces food eaten by humans, and it has done so for the entire history of humankind, and, as we have seen above, we can also thank the bee for producing the honey that fermented into our first alcoholic beverage, as the main ingredient for the honey-based mead and its variations.

We know that conservation of bees, botanicals, and all aspects of nature is a basic tenet of Druidic lore, and it is up to each of us to ensure that we do nothing to damage our living planet in any way. So it is each individual's responsibility, if they choose to engage with bee colonies, to do so in a way that honors and protects the bee, bearing in mind that bees are extremely sensitive insects that respond in a negative way to clumsy or intrusive behavior. We must never do anything to upset the delicate balance of the bee colony or to interfere with the lives of the bees that make the hive their home.

NINE

Building a Physic Garden

In this chapter, we shall look at the plants and, in particular, the flowers that established their magical reputation in the simple gardens of the common folk, the carefully cultivated gardens of the wise-women, and the magical spiritual gardens of the Druids, to whom we owe a huge debt of gratitude for their unbroken tradition and wealth of arcane knowledge that continues to inform the enchanting practice of Druidic flower magic up until the present day and beyond.

IDEAL PLANTINGS:
FUNCTIONS AND POLLINATION

As with the planning of any successful garden, the first task is to determine which plants to include in your garden stock. This may be done by considering the following criteria:

1. What spiritual or practical areas do you wish to practice in, and what circumstances do you intend to respond to?
2. What is the terroir in which you will be growing the plants?
3. What seasons do you intend to be practicing during?
4. How wide a range of plants and flowers will be practical for you to grow, maintain, and work with?

5. What volume of workings, rituals, and ceremonies is intended and are sufficient storage facilities available for this volume of crafted essences, potions, and philters?

Answering these five questions will help you determine what specific species are most appropriate and how many plants of each will be planted. It is only when you arrive at this stage that you may plan the physical layout of the physic garden, its maintenance, and the harvesting of its products. It is important then that we look at each of these stages in detail.

***Question 1.** What spiritual or practical areas do you wish to practice in, and what circumstances do you intend to respond to?*

Although it is incumbent upon each Druid to learn as many aspects of Druidic lore as is possible, many choose to practice in specific areas that suit their individual gifts the best. While most would involve themselves in generic skills, such as healing, divination, and magic crafts, most find that specific practices best match their personal gifts, skills, and abilities. When considering establishing a Druidic physic garden, you should decide upon the areas of practice for which you intend to use the produce of your garden, remembering that in this instance we are planning a spiritual physic garden comprising a collection of flowering plants to use in spiritual workings and not a healing or medicinal garden, which would look very different and contain a collection of healing herbs where the intention would be to use them in a mundane curative manner by crafting medicines, ointments, and elixirs, intending to effect a cure on a physical level.

For example, if your intention is to influence personal relationships, love, attraction, friendships, and the like, then you should refer to the flower directory that follows and select a collection of flowering plants that display attributes in those areas, whereas if you wish to work in the area of sex magic, sexual elixirs, and amatory essences, then you would select a completely different range of flowering plants. Many Druids find themselves being asked to reverse the effects of curses or lift the

evil intentions of others, and to do this they would select a specific collection of flowering plants, while others who may have been asked to
cast protective boundaries about a person or place would choose a very
different collection of plants.

In practice, of course, most Druids practice a range of disciplines,
be it large or small, and as a result most physic gardens have smaller
sections devoted to flowering plants used for different purposes. But
whether you choose to plan a physic garden for a single discipline or for
a range of practices, it is important that the intended uses are clearly
defined so that you select the correct flowering plants.

Question 2. *What is the terroir in which you will be growing the plants?*

All plants thrive better in some terroirs than they do in others; in some
cases, specific plants will not grow at all if the terroir is unsuitable.
Terroir, as noted earlier, refers to all the interacting conditions in which
the plant is growing: soil type, pH level, temperature range, rainfall level,
soil moisture and water retention, altitude, and seasonal changes. As we
are particularly concerned with flowering plants, seasonal changes like
temperature variations, day length, rainfall, and so on play a major role in
the flowering dates and length of time the blooms remain on the plants
or even if the plant flowers at all. The particular needs of each flowering
plant vary considerably, and often the best source of information on individual species is available from a seed or plant supplier, gardening books,
online resources, or even the seed packets themselves. Though many of
the plants listed in the flower directory grow throughout most of Europe
and North America, they may be difficult to find in particular regions,
such as Southern Europe or parts of the American South. In this case, it
is advisable for you to explore the spiritual attributes of the native plants
of your home region and select flowering plants that have the same or
similar characteristics to the ones listed.

It is important to note, however, that the listed flowering plants are
those that are a historical part of the Druidic tradition, so it may be necessary to conduct experimental workings to develop local substitutes. A further important consideration is that all the flowering plants listed in the

directory grow in the wild, though some may have also been cultivated as decorative flowers. As a result, it may not be easy to purchase seeds or seedlings or mature plants from commercial garden suppliers, and it may be necessary to source specialist suppliers who supply wild species seeds or rewilding suppliers online. But remember, no matter how easily you may be able to obtain seeds or seedlings of the listed plants, if they are from suppliers or individuals outside your local region, there may be legal restrictions to the species you may buy, and if your particular terroir is not suitable for the plant, they simply will not grow or flower.

Question 3. What seasons do you intend to practice during?

Even within the range of wild flowering plants listed in the directory, many will bloom at different times of the year and will remain in flower for differing periods of time, varying from those that only hold their flowers for four to six weeks to those that are more or less in constant bloom. This being the case, it is advisable to plan the garden's flowering plants so that they come into bloom at a date or season that is best suited to your area of practice. At the end of this chapter, the reader will find a list of appropriate flowering plants extracted from the directory, showing the season and dates that we would expect them to *first* bloom—bearing in mind these dates are for Northwestern Europe. Referring to the listing in the flower directory will give a guide to the period of time that the plant will normally remain in flower. Selecting the flowering plants that remain in bloom during the expected harvesting dates allows the practitioner to plan their harvesting and subsequent workings to best effect. We have seen that all flowers *must* be used as soon as possible after they are harvested, while they still retain the vital energies we need for our workings, so planning harvesting forages is imperative. Thankfully, this is easier to do in your own physic garden than it is in the wild.

Question 4. How wide a range of plants and flowers will be practical for you to grow, maintain, and work with?

No matter how well it may be planned, every physic garden will be limited by a number of constraints. Two of the most restrictive features are the size and shape of the garden and the amount of time, money, and effort the practitioner can invest in the garden. It is always important to remember that once the range of flowering plants has been identified, the physic garden layout planned, and your precious seeds or seedlings have been sown or planted, the garden and its population of plants have to be regularly maintained. This will include regular watering, thinning out, replanting, fertilizing, feeding, weeding, and so on, and all this can easily become a full-time job, consuming valuable hours every day. So when planning your physic garden, be careful not to be too ambitious with size, plant numbers, or workload. Plan to plant only the variety of species and number of plants that you can initially maintain and work with, bearing in mind that, if this is your first attempt, you need to bake in time for you to gain experience and climb the learning curve as you go. It is much more satisfying to be planning to expand your garden at the end of your first year rather than to be pulling out the remnants of unused plants and adding rotting flower heads to your compost bin.

Question 5. What volume of workings, rituals, and ceremonies is intended, and are sufficient storage facilities available for this volume of crafted essences, potions, and philters?

There is no real point in growing and harvesting more flowers than you are able to craft into potions, philters, and so on. This only results in frustration, unnecessary expense, wasted energy, and an ever-growing compost heap. So when planning the garden, think carefully about what you intend to achieve during the blooming season(s).

It may be more productive to plant a wide variety of species but just a few plants for each species, giving you the opportunity to experiment with a wide range of crafted products and explore their outcomes. However, if this garden is your first venture, it is generally advisable to err on the side of caution and plant fewer, rather than more, varieties and avoid overpopulating your physic garden. If you intend to work with only a limited variety of flowers, then plant sufficient numbers of each variety to suit your planned workings. In the same way, it is important to consider the storage of all the potions, philters, and so on that you plan to craft, as well as making sure you have sufficient bottles, jars, and such to contain them.

Bear in mind that you will always have total control of the provenance of all the flowering plants you grow in your physic garden. With careful observation of the natural world that surrounds you, it may also be possible to forage for any additional flowers you need in the wild while remembering all of the identification and harvesting criteria covered in chapter 4.

KEEPING BEES

Depending on the flowering plants you have selected, some will be annuals, flowering once a year; some biannual, flowering twice a year; some biennial, flowering once every two years; and some perennial, enduring or continually recurring. Whatever their growing cycle may be, one essential element in the life cycle of all flowering plants is pollination. In virtually all of the flowering plants used in the Druidic flower magic tradition, pollination occurs by bee pollination.

As bees visit plants in search of food, pollen attaches itself to their bodies and is then passed among plants as the bees continue to forage, fertilizing them as they go. As they gather pollen to stock their nests, bees become the most effective pollinators we know. During their repeated forays in search of pollen and nectar, each bee will travel many miles and visit hundreds of thousands of individual flowers on her journey, and as there are in the region of two billion bees on the Isles of Britain alone, we can see that the capacity for pollination is huge. It is essential to any garden that provision is made to enable the bee population to easily visit and pollinate the flowers, and this is one of the reasons for the close relationship between beekeeping and herbal or physic gardens and why every monastery that has a physic garden also has a collection of beehives and a resident beekeeper or two.

In an ideal situation, I would recommend that everyone planning a physic garden also consider keeping one or more beehives nearby. Advice on beekeeping and beekeeping supplies are readily available everywhere, and most regions have a beekeeping group or society that will nearly always welcome any inquiries and advice on establishing a hive and colony and point you toward the best local suppliers and resources. As mentioned earlier, Druids who choose to grow a physic garden will inevitably be beekeepers as well. The link between Druids, bees, and flower magic has lasted for millennia and is inherent in the core tenets of Druidic lore.

COMPANION PLANTING

We saw earlier that when harvesting flowers in the wild we must always consider the attributes of the plants that grow in close proximity to the individual plant concerned, and the influence these may have upon the virtues and attributes of the flower we intend to harvest. As you would expect, these influences may be negative or positive, or, in very few cases, benign. When planning a physic garden, we must, of course, be aware of any negative influences, as these should be avoided at all costs. For example, if we were to plant forget-me-nots, whose attributes include binding, relationships, aphrodisiacs, and the crafting of sexual elixirs and amatory essences (see the flower directory in chapter 10), in close association with fox-and-cubs, which has the attributes of dislike, animosity, conflict, and betrayal, the conflicting attributes would at best cancel each other out. If the fox-and-cubs's influence were to overpower the forget-me-nots, we could be in the position of trying to conduct a working intended to increase and bind affection while using a potion whose attributes are dislike and betrayal. In this instance, the outcome would be very uncertain but definitely not the one intended. Although we may be using only the forget-me-not flower, it will have absorbed the attributes of its neighboring fox-and-cubs as it was growing. The intensity of the fox-and-cubs's influence will depend upon just how close the two plants were when they grew. If their roots and foliage became intertwined, then neither plant would contain the expected attributes. As with everything in nature, negative associations are equally balanced by opposing positive associations, with the result that two plants with opposing attributes growing adjacent to each other cancel each other out.

The powerful way adjacent plants influence each other can be utilized in a very practical way as we plan the location of each plant in the physic garden. In the same way that adjacent plants with contradictory attributes can have a negative influence on each other, plants that share the same or complementary attributes can benefit in all sorts of ways when planted close together. In a technique known as complementary planting, we deliberately plant selected varieties so closely together that their roots and foliage intertwine, and each influences the other in a known and controlled way. For example, we could plant the same forget-me-nots in close proximity to hawthorn, which has the attributes of love, purity, binding, and cleansing. In this case, the two flowering plants not only complement each other but also reinforce and amplify the intended relationship by adding love, purity, and binding to the attributes of relationships, sexual attraction, and sexual energy in a way that most people would find beneficial.

As you can imagine, the effects of the various combinations of complementary planting may be subtle or very forceful and powerful, and the combinations are almost infinite in their variety. By growing in this way and combining the results in complex potions, as described previously, we can craft potions for almost every eventuality. From love philters to curse potions, from binding workings to casting Druid's breath, we can craft potions, powders, ointments, and other concoctions using an infinite palette of flowering plants with their virtues and influences.

Having said all that, in nature the various forces of wind, rain, soil, and so on combine to influence how individual seeds arrive at the location where they eventually grow, and some Druids allow their physic gardens to revert entirely to this complex natural process by simply rewilding, allowing nature to take its course. In this book, however, we are focused on planning, planting, and maintaining a physic garden so that we may control its population and have the greatest variety and quantity of the flowers we need for our workings at hand, as and when we need them.

PROPOSED LAYOUT OF A NEW PHYSIC GARDEN

The proposed physic garden includes twelve flowering plants, each having only positive attributes. The plants have been selected so that no matter what the season may be, there will always be some variety of flower in bloom. The collection, alphabetized by common name, is as follows:

⇜ Anemone, wood (*Anemone nemorosa*)

Flowers: March to May
Ascribed attributes: good fortune, attraction, health

⇜ Betony (*Betonica officinalis*)

Flowers: June to September
Ascribed attributes: good health, healing, vitality, goodwill

⇜ Chamomile (*Chamaemelum nobile*)

Flowers: June to September
Ascribed attributes: gentleness, tenderness, consideration

⇜ Daisy (*Bellis perennis*)

Flowers: March to October
Ascribed attributes: love, lust, physical attraction

⇜ Evening primrose, large-flowered (*Oenothera glazioviana*)

Flowers: June to October
Ascribed attributes: calm, relaxation, self-awareness

⇜ Forget-me-not, field (*Myosotis arvensis*)

Flowers: April to October
Ascribed attributes: binding, relationships (ingredient in aphrodisiacs, sexual elixirs, amatory essences)

⇜ Marigold, corn (*Glebionis segetum*)

Flowers: May to November
Ascribed attributes: joy, goodwill, well-being, security

⁂ Mint, corn (*Mentha arvensis*)

Flowers: August to September
Ascribed attributes: cleansing, purification, initiation, birth

⁂ Primrose (*Primula vulgaris*)

Flowers: March to June
Ascribed attributes: love, affection, care, commitment

⁂ Sage, wood (*Teucrium scorodonia*)

Flowers: July to October
Ascribed attributes: wisdom, learning, understanding, knowledge

⁂ Valerian, common (*Valeriana officinalis*)

Flowers: June to October
Ascribed attributes: healing, memory, knowledge, wisdom

⁂ Violet, sweet (*Viola odorata*)

Flowers: February to June
Ascribed attributes: well-being, good humor, attraction, love

Depending upon where you may be located, precise planting and growing instructions will be available from your supplier. Be careful about following instructions printed on packaging, particularly if the seeds or seedlings are not from a local source, as they may refer to different climate, soil type, or other conditions than you may be planting in.

By looking at the attributes ascribed to each plant (as shown above and again in the flower directory in chapter 10), any useful companion planting may be planned long before the garden is planted. Carefully planning the locations of the individual plants in relation to their blooming periods will also ensure that the right flowers are available when they are needed. It is also worth taking into consideration that some plants, such as mint, grow more vigorously than others and can, if not controlled correctly, spread over successive seasons to invade areas of the garden allocated to other plants. In such cases, it is important to be aware of the individual growing seasons and when each plant goes to seed. Remember, a weed is only a plant that is growing where it is not wanted, and some very productive plants can quickly turn from a beneficial asset to a pernicious, invasive weed in just a few seasons.

Below is a more comprehensive list of flowering plants arranged by the order in which they flower, which provides a broader selection that could (and should) be included in a typical physic garden.

FLOWERING PLANTS ARRANGED BY MONTH

January to March

Anemone, wood	*Anemone nemorosa*
Coltsfoot	*Tussilago farfara*
Daisy	*Bellis perennis*
Daisy, oxeye	*Leucanthemum vulgare*
Dandelion	*Taraxacum officinale*
Flax, fairy	*Linum catharticum*
Groundsel	*Senecio vulgaris*
Juniper	*Juniperus communis*
Mistletoe	*Viscum album*
Mouse-ear, common	*Cerastium fontanum*
Pimpernel, scarlet	*Anagallis arvensis*
Primrose	*Primula vulgaris*
Ramsons	*Allium ursinum*
Snowdrop	*Galanthus nivalis*
Sorrel, common	*Rumex acetosa*
Strawberry, wild	*Fragaria vesca*
Violet, sweet	*Viola odorata*

April to June

Agrimony	*Agrimonia eupatoria*
Alkanet	*Pentaglottis sempervirens*
Bird's-foot-trefoil, common	*Lotus corniculatus*
Bitter vetch	*Lathyrus linifolius*
Bluebell	*Hyacinthoides non-scripta*
Bog myrtle	*Myrica gale*
Broom	*Cytisus scoparius*

Buttercup, meadow	*Ranunculus acris*
Campion, red	*Silene dioica*
Clary, wild	*Salvia verbenaca* ssp. *horminoides*
Columbine	*Aquilegia vulgaris*
Comfrey, common	*Symphytum officinale*
Cowslip	*Primula veris*
Elder, dwarf	*Sambucus ebulus*
Enchanter's nightshade	*Circaea lutetiana*
Eyebright	*Euphrasia officinalis*
Fennel	*Foeniculum vulgare*
Field rose	*Rosa arvensis*
Forget-me-not, field	*Myosotis arvensis*
Goatsbeard	*Tragopogon pratensis*
Hawthorn	*Crataegus monogyna*
Hemlock	*Conium maculatum*
Henbane	*Hyoscyamus niger*
Honesty	*Lunaria annua*
Iris, yellow	*Iris pseudacorus*
Lady's mantle	*Alchemilla vulgaris*
Little robin	*Geranium purpureum*
Lords-and-ladies	*Arum maculatum*
Madder, wild	*Rubia peregrina*
Mallow, common	*Malva sylvestris*
Marigold, corn	*Glebionis segetum*
Marigold, marsh	*Caltha palustris*
Marsh orchid, Kerry	*Dactylorhiza kerryensis*
Meadowsweet	*Filipendula ulmaria*
Milkwort, common	*Polygala vulgaris*
Mugwort	*Artemisia vulgaris*
Mullein, great	*Verbascum thapsus*
Navelwort	*Umbilicus rupestris*
Nightshade, black	*Solanum nigrum*
Orchid, bog	*Hammarbya paludosa*
Ragged robin	*Silene flos-cuculi*
Scabious, devil's-bit	*Succisa pratensis*
Scurvygrass, common	*Cochlearia officinalis*
Self-heal	*Prunella vulgaris*
Spearwort, lesser	*Ranunculus flammula*
Speedwell, heath	*Veronica officinalis*

St. John's wort, marsh	*Hypericum elodes*
Stitchwort, greater	*Stellaria holostea*
Stonecrop, English	*Sedum anglicum*
Thyme, common	*Thymus vulgaris*
Thyme, wild	*Thymus drucei*
Toothwort	*Lathraea squamaria*
Valerian, common	*Valeriana officinalis*
Vervain	*Verbena officinalis*
Vetch, common	*Vicia sativa* ssp. *segetalis*
Water crowfoot, common	*Ranunculus aquatilis*
Water lily, white	*Nymphaea alba*
Water lily, yellow	*Nuphar lutea*
Woodruff	*Galium odoratum*
Wormwood	*Artemisia absinthium*
Woundwort, marsh	*Stachys palustris*
Yarrow	*Achillea millefolium*
Yellowwort	*Blackstonia perfoliata*

July to September

Avens, wood	*Geum urbanum*
Betony	*Betonica officinalis*
Brooklime	*Veronica beccabunga*
Buckthorn	*Rhamnus cathartica*
Burdock, lesser	*Arctium minus*
Celandine, greater	*Chelidonium majus*
Chamomile	*Chamaemelum nobile*
Cleavers	*Galium aparine*
Crowfoot, round-leaved	*Ranunculus omiophyllus*
Dog rose	*Rosa canina*
Elecampane	*Inula helenium*
Evening primrose, large-flowered	*Oenothera glazioviana*
Fat Hen	*Chenopodium album*
Foxglove	*Digitalis purpurea*
Gentian, field	*Gentianella campestris*
Goldenrod	*Solidago virgaurea*
Gypsywort	*Lycopus europaeus*
Harebell	*Campanula rotundifolia*
Heather	*Calluna vulgaris*

Helleborine, marsh	*Epipactis palustris*
Honeysuckle	*Lonicera periclymenum*
Knapweed, common	*Centaurea nigra*
Meadow rue, common	*Thalictrum flavum*
Melilot	*Melilotus officinalis*
Mint, corn	*Mentha arvensis*
Oxtongue, bristly	*Helminthotheca echioides*
Pennywort, marsh	*Hydrocotyle vulgaris*
Poppy, Welsh	*Papaver cambricum*
Ragwort, common	*Jacobaea vulgaris*
Sage, wood	*Teucrium scorodonia*
Skullcap, lesser	*Scutellaria minor*
Sneezewort	*Achillea ptarmica*
Soapwort	*Saponaria officinalis*
Sow thistle, perennial	*Sonchus arvensis*
Tansy	*Tanacetum vulgare*
Teasel, wild	*Dipsacus fullonum*
Toadflax, common	*Linaria vulgaris*

October to December

Ivy, Atlantic	*Hedera hibernica*
Shepherd's purse	*Capsella bursa-pastoris*

TEN

Directory
The Attributes of
149 Flowering Plants

The following plants are indigenous to the regions of the British Isles and Northern Europe where Druidic flower magic has been practiced for millennia. Many of these plants are also native to other geographic regions where they may be accompanied by species not included in this directory. Those species may possess equally influential spiritual essences and magical properties. It is essential that every potential practitioner consult local directories and field guides both to accurately identify regional flowering plants and to explore their spiritual energies and folkloric uses. Further worthwhile information may be garnered by researching local and regional folklore and natural magic traditions, where the practitioner may discover many valuable insights into indigenous plants and their traditional uses. Consideration should also be given to using flowering plants not listed here but that have comparable attributes. When it comes to substitutions, keep a careful record of effects and outcomes, and abide by the principles and methods of Druidic flower magic outlined in this book.

A

⟫ Agrimony (*Agrimonia eupatoria*)

Irish: *marbhdhraighean* (living flower, flower of the mortals)
Welsh: *llysiau'r drwy* (wayside vegetable or herb)
Flowers: May to September
Ascribed attributes: growth, regeneration

⟫ Alkanet (*Pentaglottis sempervirens*)

Irish: *boglas Spáineach* (Spanish boglas)
Welsh: *alkanet* (no translation)
Flowers: April to July
Ascribed attributes: travel, protection, safety

⟫ Anemone, wood (*Anemone nemorosa*)

Irish: *nead cailleach* (witch's nest)
Welsh: *blodyn y gwynt* (flower of the wind)
Flowers: March to May
Ascribed attributes: good fortune, attraction, health

⟫ Asphodel, bog (*Narthecium ossifragum*)

Irish: *sciollam na móna* (scholar of the turf)
Welsh: *llafn y bladur* (bladder blade)
Flowers: July to August
Ascribed attributes: knowledge, wisdom, fire, preservation

⟫ Aster, sea (*Tripolium pannonicum*)

Irish: *luibh bhléine* (blond, fresh herb)
Welsh: *seren y morfa* (star of the sea)
Flowers: July to October
Ascribed attributes: youth, vitality, inspiration, exposition

⟫ Avens, wood (*Geum urbanum*)

Irish: *machall coille* (wood machall)
Welsh: *mapgoll* (no translation)
Flowers: July to October
Ascribed attributes: secrecy, talent, hidden affection

B

⚘ Betony (*Betonica officinalis*)

Irish: *lus beatha* (herb of life)
Welsh: *cribau San Ffraid* (Saint Bride's cribs)
Flowers: June to September
Ascribed attributes: good health, healing, vitality, goodwill

⚘ Bindweed, field (*Convolvulus arvensis*)

Irish: *ainleog* (no translation)
Welsh: *cwlwm y Cythrael* (knot of Israel)
Flowers: July to September
Ascribed attributes: attraction, binding, security, protection

⚘ Bird's-foot-trefoil, common (*Lotus corniculatus*)

Irish: *crobh éin* (bird's feathers)
Welsh: *troid yr aderyn* (bird's foot)
Flowers: June to September
Ascribed attributes: happiness, energy, determination

⚘ Bistort, amphibious (*Persicaria amphibia*)

Irish: *glúineach uisce* (dipping water)
Welsh: *canwraidd y dwr* (water bird or canary)
Flowers: June to September
Ascribed attributes: aggression, loss, resentment, hatred

⚘ Bitter cress, hairy (*Cardamine hirsuta*)

Irish: *searbh-bhiolar giobach* (sharp bitter cress)
Welsh: *chwerw blewog* (hairy bitter cress)
Flowers: February to November
Ascribed attributes: anger, violence, grievance, dispute

⚘ Bitter vetch (*Lathyrus linifolius*)

Irish: *corra meille* (no translation)
Welsh: *ytbysen y coed* (wood ash)
Flowers: April to July
Ascribed attributes: vengeance, hatred, danger

⚘ Bluebell (*Hyacinthoides non-scripta*)

Irish: *coinnle corra* (old candles)
Welsh: *clychau'r gog* (blue bells)

Flowers: April to May
Ascribed attributes: well-being, health, cooperation, vitality

✺ Bog myrtle (*Myrica gale*)

Irish: *roideóg* (no translation)
Welsh: *helygen Mair* (willow Mary)
Flowers: April to May
Ascribed attributes: other realms, travel, dreams, imagination, creativity

✺ Brooklime (*Veronica beccabunga*)

Irish: *lochall* (no translation)
Welsh: *calch nant* (brook lime)
Flowers: May to September
Ascribed attributes: security, trust, bonding

✺ Brookweed (*Samolus valerandi*)

Irish: *falcaire uisce* (water cleanser)
Welsh: *claerlys* (brookweed)
Flowers: May to September
Ascribed attributes: cleansing, reversing failure, success, good fortune

✺ Broom (*Cytisus scoparius*)

Irish: *giolcach shléibhe* (mountain reed)
Welsh: *banhadlen* (broom or brush)
Flowers: April to May
Ascribed attributes: good fortune, new beginning, cleansing

✺ Buckthorn (*Rhamnus cathartica*)

Irish: *paide bréan* (foul breath)
Welsh: *rhafnwydden* (rope or harness)
Flowers: May to June
Ascribed attributes: purging, cleansing

✺ Bugloss (*Lycopsis arvensis*)

Irish: *boglas* (no translation)
Welsh: *bleidd-drem* (wolf hound)
Flowers: April to September
Ascribed attributes: friendship, affection, care

✺ Burdock, lesser (*Arctium minus*)

Irish: *cnádán* (card thistle)
Welsh: *cyngaf bychan* (small harvest)

Flowers: July to September
Ascribed attributes: cleansing, purging, healing

ᚘ Buttercup, meadow (*Ranunculus acris*)

Irish: *fearbán féir* (grassy buttercup)
Scottish: *buidheag-an-t-samhraidh* (little yellow of the summer)
Welsh: *blodyn y menyn* (butter flower)
Flowers: April to October
Ascribed attributes: love, attraction, wholesomeness

C

ᚘ Campion, red (*Silene dioica*)

Irish: *coireán coilleach* (no translation)
Welsh: *blodyn taranau* (thunder flower)
Flowers: April to August
Ascribed attributes: power, vitality, longevity

ᚘ Cat's ear (*Hypochaeris radicata*)

Irish: *cluas chait* (cat's ear)
Welsh: *lust y gath* (cat's ear)
Flowers: June to September
Ascribed attributes: intelligence, wisdom, learning

ᚘ Celandine, greater (*Chelidonium majus*)

Irish: *garra bhui* (no translation)
Welsh: *dilwydd* (no translation)
Flowers: April to October
Ascribed attributes: happiness, well-being

ᚘ Centaury, common (*Centaurium erythraea*)

Irish: *dréimire Mhuire* (Mary's ladder)
Welsh: *busti y ddae* (no translation)
Flowers: June to September
Ascribed attributes: the unknown, other realms, divination

ᚘ Chamomile (*Chamaemelum nobile*)

Irish: *camán meal* (no translation)
Welsh: *camri* (no translation)
Flowers: June to September
Ascribed attributes: gentleness, tenderness, consideration

ᙗ Cinquefoil, marsh (*Comarum palustre*)

Irish: *cnó léana* (meadow nut)
Welsh: *pumdalen y gors* (five petal of the marsh)
Flowers: June to September
Ascribed attributes: health, well-being, light, illumination

ᙗ Clary, wild (*Salvia verbenaca* ssp. *horminoides*)

Irish: *tormán* (storm flower)
Welsh: *saets gwyllt* (festival sage)
Flowers: May to August
Ascribed attributes: wisdom, knowledge, intelligence

ᙗ Cleavers (*Galium aparine*)

Irish: *garbhlus* (goose grass)
Welsh: *llau'r offeiriad* (priest's eyes)
Flowers: May to September
Ascribed attributes: devotion, friendship, community

ᙗ Clover, red (*Trifolium pratense*)

Irish: *seamair dhearg* (red clover)
Welsh: *meillionen goch* (red clover)
Flowers: May to October
Ascribed attributes: love, passion, lust, physical desire

ᙗ Coltsfoot (*Tussilago farfara*)

Irish: *sponc* (no translation)
Welsh: *carn yr ebol* (colt's foot)
Flowers: May to February
Ascribed attributes: attraction, good fortune, binding, desire

ᙗ Columbine (*Aquilegia vulgaris*)

Irish: *colaimbín* (columbine)
Welsh: *blodau'r sipsi* (gypsy's flower)
Flowers: May to July
Ascribed attributes: motherhood, enhancing childbirth, future prosperity

ᙗ Comfrey, common (*Symphytum officinale*)

Irish: *lus na gcnámh mbriste* (plant of the broken bone)
Welsh: *dail cwmffri* (comfrey leaves)
Flowers: May to July
Ascribed attributes: healing, well-being, vitality.

❧ Cowslip (*Primula veris*)

Irish: *bainne bó bleachtáin* (cow's milk weed)
Welsh: *briallu Mair* (Mary's primrose)
Flowers: April and May
Ascribed attributes: youth, energy, virility, power

❧ Creeping Jenny (*Lysimachia nummularia*)

Irish: *lus an dá phingin* (tuppenny flower)
Welsh: *Siani lusg* (creeping Jenny)
Flowers: June to August
Ascribed attributes: joy, happiness, energy

❧ Crowfoot, round-leaved (*Ranunculus omiophyllus*)

Irish: *néal uisce cruinn* (powerful water cleanser)
Welsh: *egyllt y rhosdir* (wing of the moorland)
Flowers: May to August
Ascribed attributes: purity, cleansing, water-based energies

❧ Cuckoo flower (*Cardamine pratensis*)

Irish: *biolar gréagháin* (cuckoo flower)
Welsh: *blodyn y gog* (cuckoo's flower)
Flowers: April to June
Ascribed attributes: affection, attraction, binding, new beginning

D

❧ Daisy (*Bellis perennis*)

Irish: *nóinín* (daisy)
Welsh: *llygad y dydd* (eye of the day)
Flowers: March to October
Ascribed attributes: love, lust, physical attraction

❧ Daisy, oxeye (*Leucanthemum vulgare*)

Irish: *nóinín mór* (large daisy)
Welsh: *llygad llo* (calf's eye)
Flowers: March to September
Ascribed attribute: physical attraction

❧ Dandelion (*Taraxacum officinale*)

Irish: *bior na bríde* (lance of the maiden)
Scottish: *fiacal leomhann* (lion's tooth)

Welsh: *dant y llew* (tooth of the lion)
Flowers: March to October
Ascribed attributes: love, affection, physical desire, lust, sexual stimulation

❀ Dewberry (*Rubus caesius*)

Irish: *eithreog* (dewberry)
Welsh: *llwyn mwyar Mair* (Mary's black berry bush)
Flowers: June and July
Ascribed attributes: envy, lust, hatred, ill-wishes

❀ Dog rose (*Rosa canina*)

Irish: *feirdhris* (no translation)
Welsh: *rhosyn gwyllt* (wild rose)
Flowers: June to August
Ascribed attributes: love, binding, physical attraction

❀ Dropwort (*Filipendula vulgaris*)

Irish: *lus braonach* (dripping weed)
Welsh: *crogedyf* (pendant herb)
Flowers: March to August
Ascribed attributes: healing, well-being, good health

E

❀ Elder (*Sambucus nigra*)

Irish: *trom* (no translation)
Welsh: *ysgawen* (elder)
Flowers: May and June
Ascribed attributes: knowledge, wisdom, learning

❀ Elder, dwarf (*Sambucus ebulus*)

Irish: *tromán* (no translation)
Welsh: *ysgawen fair* (fair elder)
Flowers: June to September
Ascribed attributes: beauty, attraction, goodwill

❀ Elecampane (*Inula helenium*)

Irish: *meacan aillinn* (no translation)
Welsh: *marchalan* (no translation)
Flowers: July to September
Ascribed attributes: well-being, good health, recovery

⇻ Enchanter's nightshade (*Circaea lutetiana*)

Irish: *fuinseagach* (no translation)
Welsh: *llysiau Steffan* (Stephen's flower)
Flowers: May to September
Ascribed attributes: the otherworld, mystery, magic

⇻ Evening primrose, large-flowered (*Oenothera glazioviana*)

Irish: *coinneal oíche mhór* (large night candle)
Welsh: *briallu* (primrose)
Flowers: June to October
Ascribed attributes: calm, relaxation, self-awareness

⇻ Eyebright (*Euphrasia officinalis*)

Irish: *glanrose* (no translation)
Welsh: *effros* (no translation)
Flowers: June to October
Ascribed attributes: clarity, divination, foresight, preparation

F

⇻ Fat hen (*Chenopodium album*)

Irish: *praiseach fhiáin* (wild tangled flowers)
Welsh: *tafod yr oen* (lamb's tongue)
Flowers: June to November
Ascribed attributes: cleansing, purity, innocence, naivete

⇻ Fennel (*Foeniculum vulgare*)

Irish: *finéal* (fennel)
Welsh: *ffenigl cyffredin* (wild fennel)
Flowers: June to November
Ascribed attributes: clarity, vision, insight, understanding

⇻ Figwort, common (*Scrophularia nodosa*)

Irish: *donnlus* (no translation)
Welsh: *gornerth* (no translation)
Flowers: July to October
Ascribed attributes: knowledge, learning, discovery

⇻ Flax, fairy (*Linum catharticum*)

Irish: *lus na mban sí* (lady's flower)
Welsh: *llin y tylwyth teg* (flax of the fair people [fairies])

Flowers: March to October
Ascribed attributes: communication with the otherworld, insight, vision

ᴥ Forget-me-not, field (*Myosotis arvensis*)

Irish: *lus mionla goirt* (salty herb)
Scottish: *dìochuimhnich-mi-chan* (no translation)
Welsh: *ysgorpionllys y meusydd* (unhappy partner)
Flowers: April to October
Ascribed attributes: binding, relationships

ᴥ Fox-and-cubs (*Pilosella aurantiaca*)

Irish: *dearbh dhearg* (bitter red herb)
Welsh: *llwynog a chybiau* (fox-and-cubs)
Flowers: June to September
Ascribed attributes: dislike, animosity, conflict, betrayal

ᴥ Foxglove (*Digitalis purpurea*)

Irish: *lus mór* (great flower)
Welsh: *bysedd y cŵ* (dog's fingers)
Flowers: June to September
Ascribed attributes: bad outcomes, failure, disappointment, loss

G

ᴥ Gentian, field (*Gentianella campestris*)

Irish: *lus an chrúbáin* (horse hooves plant)
Welsh: *crwynllys y meas* (gentle herb of the field)
Flowers: July to November
Ascribed attributes: delicacy, fragility, gracefulness, caring

ᴥ Goatsbeard (*Tragopogon pratensis*)

Irish: *finidí na muc* (little piglets)
Welsh: *barf yr afr felen* (yellow goat beard)
Flowers: June to September
Ascribed attributes: distress, upset, confusion

ᴥ Goldenrod (*Solidago virgaurea*)

Irish: *slat óir* (gold rod)
Welsh: *aurwialen* (gold staff)
Flowers: July to October
Ascribed attributes: power, authority, pity, forgiveness

⚘ Gorse (*Ulex europaeus*)

Irish: *aiteann Gallda* (Gaelic gorse)
Welsh: *eithne Ffrengig* (French gorse)
Flowers: January to December
Ascribed attributes: protection, safety, banishment

⚘ Groundsel (*Senecio vulgaris*)

Irish: *grúnlas* (groundsel)
Welsh: *creulys cyffredin* (groundsel)
Flowers: January to December
Ascribed attributes: healing, relief of pain, comfort

⚘ Gypsywort (*Lycopus europaeus*)

Irish: *feorán corraigh* (moving grass)
Welsh: *perlysiau sipsiwn* (gypsy herb)
Flowers: July to August
Ascribed attributes: celebration, mystery, foresight, travel

H

⚘ Harebell (*Campanula rotundifolia*)

Irish: *méaracán gorm* (blue thistle)
Welsh: *cloch ysgyfarnog* (bell hare)
Flowers: July to November
Ascribed attributes: affection, communication, warning, foresight

⚘ Hawthorn (*Crataegus monogyna*)

Irish: *sceach gheal* (hawthorn)
Welsh: *draenen wen* (white thorn)
Flowers: May to July
Ascribed attributes: love, purity, binding, cleansing

⚘ Heather (*Calluna vulgaris*)

Irish: *fraoch mór* (greater heather)
Welsh: *grug* (heather)
Flowers: July to November
Ascribed attributes: purity, cleansing, vitality, energy

⚘ Helleborine, marsh (*Epipactis palustris*)

Irish: *cuaichín corraigh* (no translation)
Welsh: *caldrist y gors* (marsh helleborine)

Flowers: July to September
Ascribed attributes: secrecy, concealment, confusion, distraction

✤ Hemlock (*Conium maculatum*)

Irish: *moing mhear* (fasting herb)
Welsh: *cegiden* (hemlock)
Flowers: June to August
Ascribed attributes: death, hatred, misfortune, disaster

✤ Henbane (*Hyoscyamus niger*)

Irish: *gafann* (no translation)
Welsh: *llewyg yr lâr* (falling chicken plant)
Flowers: May to September
Ascribed attributes: confusion, uncertainty, misdirection

✤ Hogweed (*Heracleum sphondylium*)

Irish: *feabhrán* (no translation)
Welsh: *panasen y cawr* (giant parsnip)
Flowers: June to October
Ascribed attributes: growth, development, maturity

✤ Honesty (*Lunaria annua*)

Irish: *lus na gealai* (moon flower)
Welsh: blodyn y lleuad (flower of the moon)
Flowers: April to July
Ascribed attributes: truth, openness, dependency, sincerity

✤ Honeysuckle (*Lonicera periclymenum*)

Irish: *féithleann* (honeysuckle)
Welsh: *gwyddfid* (honeysuckle)
Flowers: July to September
Ascribed attributes: sweetness, love, affection, kindness

✤ Hound's-tongue (*Cynoglossum officinale*)

Irish: *teanga chon* (dog's tongue)
Welsh: *tafod y ci* (dog's tongue)
Flowers: June to September
Ascribed attributes: anger, disappointment, abandonment

I

✿ Iris, yellow (*Iris pseudacorus*)
Irish: *feileastram* (no translation)
Welsh: *iris felen* (yellow iris)
Flowers: June to September
Ascribed attributes: joy, happiness, success, good fortune

✿ Ivy, Atlantic (*Hedera hibernica*)
Irish: *eidhneán* (ivy)
Welsh: *eiddew* (ivy)
Flowers: September to December
Ascribed attributes: evil, ill fortune, failure, disaster

J

✿ Juniper (*Juniperus communis*)
Irish: *aiteal* (no translation)
Welsh: *merywen* (juniper)
Flowers: March to July
Ascribed attributes: resentment, bitterness, dislike

K

✿ Knapweed, common (*Centaurea nigra*)
Irish: *minscoth* (fine petal flower)
Welsh: *pengaled* (stubborn head)
Flowers: July to November
Ascribed attributes: progress, advancement, success

✿ Knotgrass (*Polygonum aviculare*)
Irish: *gliúneach bheag* (small sticky flower)
Welsh: *canclwm* (knotgrass)
Flowers: June to December
Ascribed attributes: healing, well-being, contentment

L

✿ Lady's mantle (*Alchemilla vulgaris*)
Irish: *dearna mhuire* (our lady's mantle)
Welsh: *mantell fenyw* (lady's mantle)

Flowers: May to October
Ascribed attributes: protection, secrets, concealment

➤ Lavender, western sea (*Limonium recurvum*)
Irish: *lus liath na Boirne* (Burren gray herb)
Welsh: *lafant* (lavender)
Flowers: July to August
Ascribed attributes: purity, cleansing, relaxation, harmony; identifies infidelity

➤ Little robin (*Geranium purpureum*)
Irish: *eireaball rí* (king's tail)
Welsh: *robin fach* (small robin)
Flowers: May to November
Ascribed attributes: longevity, good health, lasting love

➤ Loosestrife, yellow (*Lysimachia vulgaris*)
Irish: *breallán léana* (meadow blanket)
Welsh: *trewynyn* (lamb's comfort)
Flowers: July to September
Ascribed attributes: cleansing, purity, youth, childbirth

➤ Lords-and-ladies (*Arum maculatum*)
Irish: *cluas chaoin* (weeping ears)
Welsh: *pidyn y gog* (cuckoo pint)
Flowers: April to June
Ascribed attributes: renewal, revival, virility, energy

➤ Lousewort (*Pedicularis sylvatica*)
Irish: *lus an ghiolla* (servant's herb)
Welsh: *melog y cŵn* (dog's honey)
Flowers: April to August
Ascribed attributes: protection, healing, cleansing

M

➤ Madder, wild (*Rubia peregrina*)
Irish: *garbhlus na Boirne* (rugged herb of the Burren)
Welsh: *cochwraidd gwyl* (wild red herb)
Flowers: June to September
Ascribed attributes: fierceness, anger, confrontation

⚜ Mallow, common (*Malva sylvestris*)

Irish: *lus na meall Muire* (Mary's herb)
Welsh: *hocys cyffredin* (common mallow)
Flowers: June to November
Ascribed attributes: healing, contentment, happiness

⚜ Marigold, corn (*Glebionis segetum*)

Irish: *buían* (yellow herb)
Welsh: *gold yr ŷd* (golden corn)
Flowers: May to November
Ascribed attributes: joy, goodwill, well-being, security

⚜ Marigold, marsh (*Caltha palustris*)

Irish: *lus bui Bealtaine* (May herb, herb of Bealtaine)
Welsh: *gold y gors* (gold of the marsh)
Flowers: April to September
Ascribed attributes: energy, vitality, enthusiasm, devotion

⚜ Marsh orchid, Kerry (*Dactylorhiza kerryensis*)

Irish: *magairlin Gaelach* (Gaelic orchid)
Welsh: *tegeirian Gwyddelig* (Gaelic orchid)
Flowers: May and June
Ascribed attributes: lust, sexual power, fertility, physical attraction

⚜ Meadow rue, common (*Thalictrum flavum*)

Irish: *rú léana* (meadow rue)
Welsh: *arianllys* (silver staff)
Flowers: July and August
Ascribed attributes: knowledge, wisdom, insight, understanding

⚜ Meadowsweet (*Filipendula ulmaria*)

Irish: *airgead luacgra* (money rushes)
Welsh: *brenhines y weirglodd* (queen of the meadow)
Flowers: June to October
Ascribed attributes: healing, health, wisdom, knowledge

⚜ Melilot (*Melilotus officinalis*)

Irish: *crúibín cait* (cat's foot)
Welsh: *pawen cath* (cat's paw)
Flowers: June to October
Ascribed attributes: travel, health, protection, reward

⤜ Milkwort, common (*Polygala vulgaris*)

Irish: *lus an bhainne* (milk herb)
Welsh: *llysiau Crist* (Christ's herb)
Flowers: May to October
Ascribed attributes: well-being, comfort, security, nurturing

⤜ Mint, corn (*Mentha arvensis*)

Irish: *mismin arbhair* (corn mint)
Welsh: *mintys yr ŷd* (corn mint)
Flowers: August and September
Ascribed attributes: cleansing, purification, initiation, birth

⤜ Mistletoe (*Viscum album*)

Irish: *sú darach* (oak juice) or *deualus* (mistletoe)
Welsh: *uchelwydd* (corn mistletoe)
Flowers: February and March
Ascribed attributes: magic, healing, the otherworld, mysticism

⤜ Mouse-ear, common (*Cerastium fontanum*)

Irish: *cluas luchóige mhara* (perpetual mouse ear)
Welsh: *clust y lygoden* (mouse's ear)
Flowers: February to December
Ascribed attributes: unfaithful, broken promises, betrayal, untrustworthy

⤜ Mugwort (*Artemisia vulgaris*)

Irish: *meisce* (mugwort)
Welsh: *beidiog lwyd* (gray beetle flower)
Flowers: May to October
Ascribed attributes: recall, memory, past times

⤜ Mullein, great (*Verbascum thapsus*)

Irish: *oinnle Muire* (candles of Mary)
Welsh: *pannog melyn* (yellow mullein)
Flowers: June to October
Ascribed attributes: faith, faithfulness, devotion, commitment

N

⤜ Navelwort (*Umbilicus rupestris*)

Irish: *cornán caisil* (chestnut cups)
Welsh: *deilen gron* (round leaf herb)

Flowers: June to October
Ascribed attributes: birth, fertility, nurture

⇒ Nightshade, black (*Solanum nigrum*)

Irish: *fuath dubh* (black hatred)
Welsh: *codwarth du* (black nightshade)
Flowers: May to October
Ascribed attributes: hatred, vengeance, retribution, dislike

⇒ Nipplewort (*Lapsana communis*)

Irish: *duilleog Bhríde* (Brigid's leaves)
Welsh: *cartheig* (no translation)
Flowers: May to November
Ascribed attributes: dependency, nurturing, maintenance, commitment

O

⇒ Orchid, bog (*Hammarbya paludosa*)

Irish: *magairlín na móna* (peat orchid)
Welsh: *tegeirian bach y gors* (little orchid from the marsh)
Flowers: July to October
Ascribed attributes: envy, absence, yearning

⇒ Oxtongue, bristly (*Helminthotheca echioides*)

Irish: *teanga bhó gharbh* (rough cow's tongue)
Welsh: *gwlaeth chwerw* (bitter witchcraft)
Flowers: June to December
Ascribed attributes: witchcraft, spite, hatred, mystery

P

⇒ Pennywort, marsh (*Hydrocotyle vulgaris*)

Irish: *lus na pingine* (penny herb)
Welsh: *ceiniog y gors* (marsh penny)
Flowers: June to September
Ascribed attributes: good fortune, wealth

⇒ Pimpernel, scarlet (*Anagallis arvensis*)

Irish: *falcaire fiain* (no translation)
Welsh: *gwlydd Mair* (Mary's dress)

Flowers: March to November
Ascribed attributes: desire, sexual attraction, lust

⚘ Poppy, common (*Papaver rhoeas*)

Irish: *cailleach dhearg* (red witch flower)
Welsh: *pabi coch* (red poppy)
Flowers: June to September
Ascribed attributes: caution, warning, restraint, self-control

⚘ Poppy, Welsh (*Papaver cambricum*)

Irish: *poipin Breatnach* (Welsh poppy)
Welsh: *pabi Cymreig* (poppy of Wales)
Flowers: June to September
Ascribed attributes: travel, absence, lost, the unknown

⚘ Primrose (*Primula vulgaris*)

Irish: *sabhaircin* (primrose)
Welsh: *beiallu* (primrose)
Flowers: March to June
Ascribed attributes: love, affection, care, commitment

R

⚘ Ragged robin (*Silene flos-cuculi*)

Irish: *lus sioda* (silky herb)
Welsh: *carpiog y gors* (ragged marsh herb)
Flowers: May to September
Ascribed attributes: happiness, joy, pleasure, goodwill

⚘ Ragwort, common (*Jacobaea vulgaris*)

Irish: *buachalán buí* (yellow boy)
Scottish: *cushag* (big stalk)
Welsh: *creulys Iago* (James's ragwort, Jacob's ragwort)
Flowers: June to December
Ascribed attributes: longevity, love, health, well-being

⚘ Ramsons (*Allium ursinum*)

Irish: *creamh* (garlic)
Welsh: *craf y geifr* (wild goat's garlic)
Flowers: April to June
Ascribed attributes: cleansing, purity, protection, banishment

⚘ Rose, field (*Rosa arvensis*)

Irish: *rós léana* (meadow rose)
Welsh: *rhosyn gwyn gwyllt* (wild white rose)
Flowers: June and July
Ascribed attributes: purity, pure love, virginity, unspoiled

⚘ Rowan (*Sorbus aucuparia*)

Irish: *caorthann* (rowan)
Welsh: *cerddinen* (whitebeam)
Flowers: May and June
Ascribed attributes: youth, vitality, energy, strength

S

⚘ Sage, wood (*Teucrium scorodonia*)

Irish: *iúr sléibhe* (small mountain yew)
Welsh: *chwerwlys eithin* (bitter gorse)
Flowers: July to October
Ascribed attributes: wisdom, learning, understanding, knowledge

⚘ Scabious, devil's bit (*Succisa pratensis*)

Irish: *odhrach ghallach* (speckled toad herb)
Welsh: *clafrllys gwreidd* (scabious root)
Flowers: June to November
Ascribed attributes: curses, vengeance, punishment, malevolence

⚘ Scurvygrass, common (*Cochlearia officinalis*)

Irish: *biolar trá* (beach cress)
Welsh: *llwylys cyffredin* (common throat herb)
Flowers: May to September
Ascribed attributes: healing, repair, reinstatement, recovery

⚘ Self-heal (*Prunella vulgaris*)

Irish: *féin leigheas* (self-heal)
Welsh: *craith unnos* (quick healing wound)
Flowers: June to September
Ascribed attributes: healing, recovery

⚘ Shepherd's purse (*Capsella bursa-pastoris*)

Irish: *lus an sparáin* (purse plant)
Welsh: *pwrs y bugail* (shepherd's purse)

Flowers: January to December
Ascribed attributes: wealth, good fortune, happiness, overcoming troubles

⤳ Skullcap, lesser (*Scutellaria minor*)

Irish: *cochall beag* (small hooded plant)
Welsh: *cycyllog* (hooded herb)
Flowers: July to November
Ascribed attributes: opportunity, chance, the unknown, the unplanned

⤳ Sneezewort (*Achillea ptarmica*)

Irish: *lus corráin* (crescent herb)
Welsh: *perlysiau tisian* (sneezing herb)
Flowers: July to October
Ascribed attributes: healing, improvement, repair, reinstatement

⤳ Snowdrop (*Galanthus nivalis*)

Irish: *plúirín sneachta* (snowflake)
Welsh: *eirlys* (snowdrop)
Flowers: January to April
Ascribed attributes: purity, cleansing, virginity, youth, new beginnings

⤳ Soapwort (*Saponaria officinalis*)

Irish: *garbhán creagach* (herb from the stones)
Welsh: *sebonllys* (soap herb)
Flowers: July to October
Ascribed attributes: cleansing, purity, virginity

⤳ Sorrel, common (*Rumex acetosa*)

Irish: *samhadh bó* (cow's sorrel)
Welsh: *suran y cŵn* (dog's sorrel)
Flowers: March to September
Ascribed attributes: protection, repulsion, guardianship

⤳ Sow thistle, perennial (*Sonchus arvensis*)

Irish: *bleachtán léana* (meadow milk herb)
Welsh: *llaethysgallen yr ŷd* (milk thistle from the cornfield)
Flowers: July to November
Ascribed attributes: nurturing, protection, encouragement, cherishing

⤳ Spearwort, lesser (*Ranunculus flammula*)

Irish: *glasair léana bheag* (small meadow herb)
Welsh: *llafnlys bach* (small lacey herb)

Flowers: May to October
Ascribed attributes: aggression, anger, hostility, injury

⋙ Speedwell, heath (*Veronica officinalis*)

Irish: *lus cré* (herb of the earth)
Welsh: *rhwyddlwyn meddygol* (soothing medicinal herb)
Flowers: May to September
Ascribed attributes: healing, soothing, comfort, nurturing

⋙ Spurge, Irish (*Euphorbia hyberna*)

Irish: *bainne caoin* (milky tears)
Welsh: *clust yr ewig* (hind's ear)
Flowers: April to July
Ascribed attributes: abundance, plenty, prosperity, justice

⋙ St. John's wort, marsh (*Hypericum elodes*)

Irish: *luibh an chiorriathe* (chrysanthemum herb)
Welsh: *Eurinllys y gors* (St. John's herb from the marsh)
Flowers: June to October
Ascribed attributes: healing, adversity, comfort, restoring

⋙ Stitchwort, greater (*Stellaria holostea*)

Irish: *tursarraing mhór* (great stitch herb)
Welsh: *serenllys mawr* (great star herb)
Flowers: April to July
Ascribed attributes: healing, binding, joining together, restoring

⋙ Stonecrop, English (*Sedum anglicum*)

Irish: *póiríní seangán* (ant purse)
Welsh: *briweg y cerrig* (small stone herb)
Flowers: June to October
Ascribed attributes: creating boundaries, establishing restrictions, new
frontiers

⋙ Strawberry, wild (*Fragaria vesca*)

Irish: *sú talún fiáin* (wild strawberry)
Welsh: *mefus gwyllt* (wild strawberry)
Flowers: April to August
Ascribed attributes: affection, friendship, consideration, love

T

⊰⊱ Tansy (*Tanacetum vulgare*)
Irish: *franclus* (tansy)
Welsh: *tanclys* (tansy)
Flowers: July to October
Ascribed attributes: humor, pleasure, goodwill, hope

⊰⊱ Teasel, wild (*Dipsacus fullonum*)
Irish: *leadán úcaire* (fuller's teasel)
Welsh: *crib y pannwr* (fuller's hooks)
Flowers: July and August
Ascribed attributes: protection, forming barriers, secrets

⊰⊱ Thistle, marsh (*Cirsium palustre*)
Irish: *feochadán corraigh* (moving thistle)
Welsh: *ysgallen y gors* (marsh thistle)
Flowers: July to October
Ascribed attributes: dislike, spite, hatred, vengeance

⊰⊱ Thyme, common (*Thymus vulgaris*)
Irish: *tím chreige* (rock thyme)
Scottish: *tìom* (thyme)
Welsh: *teim* (thyme)
Flowers: March to September
Ascribed attributes: good health, prosperity, emotional courage, lasting love

⊰⊱ Thyme, wild (*Thymus drucei*)
Irish: *tím chreige* (rock thyme)
Welsh: *gruwlys gwyllt mwyaf* (greater wild hair wort)
Flowers: June to October
Ascribed attributes: wisdom, comfort, security, knowledge

⊰⊱ Toadflax, common (*Linaria vulgaris*)
Irish: *buaflíon* (toad herb)
Welsh: *llin y lyffant* (toad wort)
Flowers: July to November
Ascribed attributes: foresight, divination, future plans

⊰⊱ Toothwort (*Lathraea squamaria*)
Irish: *slánú fiacal* (tooth healer)
Welsh: *deintlys cennog* (ailing tooth)

Flowers: April and May
Ascribed attributes: healing, comfort, relaxation, confidence

V

Valerian, common (*Valeriana officinalis*)

Irish: *caorthann corraigh* (healing herb)
Welsh: *triaglog* (valerian)
Flowers: June to October
Ascribed attributes: healing, memory, knowledge, wisdom

Vervain (*Verbena officinalis*)

Irish: beirbhéine (vervain)
Welsh: *briw'r march* (wound herb)
Flowers: June to November
Ascribed attributes: healing, relaxation, comfort

Vetch, common (*Vicia sativa* ssp. *segetalis*)

Irish: *peasair chapaill* (horse vetch)
Welsh: *ffugbysen faethol* (healing vetch herb)
Flowers: May to October
Ascribed attributes: healing, well-being, goodwill

Violet, sweet (*Viola odorata*)

Irish: *sailchuach chumhra* (fragrant violet)
Welsh: *fioled bêr* (sweet violet)
Flowers: February to June
Ascribed attributes: well-being, good humor, attraction, love

W

Water crowfoot, common (*Ranunculus aquatilis*)

Irish: *néal uisce coiteann* (common water crow's foot)
Welsh: *crafanc y dŵr* (water crow's claw)
Flowers: April to September
Ascribed attributes: traveling, adventure, the unknown, enthusiasm

Water lily, white (*Nymphaea alba*)

Irish: *bacán bán* (white water lily)
Welsh: *lili-ddŵr wen* (white water lily)
Flowers: June to September
Ascribed attributes: purity, cleansing, childbirth, fertility

⋙ Water lily, yellow (*Nuphar lutea*)

Irish: *Cabhán abhann* (Cavan river lily)
Welsh: *lili-ddŵr felen* (yellow water lily)
Flowers: June to September
Ascribed attributes: deceit, distrust, disbelief

⋙ Woodruff (*Galium odoratum*)

Irish: *lus moileas* (the bitter-sweet herb*)
Welsh: *briwydden bêr* (sweet bedstraw); also *anadl babi* (baby's breath)
Flowers: May to July
Ascribed attributes: honesty, relaxation, innocence, truth

⋙ Wormwood (*Artemisia absinthium*)

Irish: *mormónta* (wormwood)
Welsh: *wermod lwyd* (gray wormwood)
Flowers: May to September
Ascribed attributes: otherworldliness, mysticism, hidden meanings

⋙ Woundwort, marsh (*Stachys palustris*)

Irish: *cabhsadán* (no translation)
Welsh: *briwlys y gors* (healing herb of the marsh)
Flowers: June to September
Ascribed attributes: healing, repair, devotion, consideration

Y

⋙ Yarrow (*Achillea millefolium*)

Irish: *athair thalún* (father of the earth)
Welsh: *milddail* (milk wort)
Flowers: June to December
Ascribed attributes: bitterness, spite, hatred, vindictiveness

⋙ Yellowwort (*Blackstonia perfoliata*)

Irish: *dréimire buí* (yellow ladder)
Welsh: *canri felen* (yellow herb or yellow bird)
Flowers: June to November
Ascribed attributes: beauty, delicacy, well-being, happiness

---

*Not to be confused with the herb bittersweet.

An Unbroken Lineage of Practical Magic

Druidic flower magic is an accessible, practical form of magic that for many years has been overlooked in preference for more flamboyant, ceremonial forms of the art of magic. Often passed over as a delicate and gentle practice because of its dependence upon the sometimes frail but beautiful flowers that form its core tenet, the elegance and subtlety of flower magic may, in some cases, disguise its potency and vital energies.

It is not difficult to track the development of the use of flowers in magic from the pre-Celtic culture of the Grooved ware people who initially inhabited the British Isles through the various occupying cultures of the Celtic-speaking peoples, Roman invaders, the Angles and Saxons, and the final Norman conquerors who ensured the dominance of Christian beliefs, which overwhelmed the arcane beliefs of the cunning folk, wise-women, and Druids of Wales, Scotland, Ireland, and the whole of what is now England. Thankfully the important arcane beliefs and practices of flower magic have been retained by the various occult subcultures that have survived in an unbroken lineage since those ancient times.

The flower magic practices we see in today's Druidic lore, witchcraft, and simple cunning-folk tradition are directly descended from these ancient magicians through an oral tradition that is still a vital part of the many rural communities of the Isles of Britain. This tradition, which in many cases reflects the coalescing of a number of rural traditions, may be viewed with skepticism by many who may not be directly involved in the culture.

Modern society tends to underestimate the importance and accuracy of the many oral traditions that appear in the majority of ethnic cultures around the world, choosing instead to put the emphasis on pottery remains, carbon dating, visible remnants, and, in many cases, written history. While there is little to be gained by contradicting scientific fact, it is worth remembering that much of what is written about these cultures and accepted as undeniable fact is based on ancient oral history, recounted by the descendants of these cultures and recorded by contemporary historians. But these historians had their own agendas and prejudices, which is very apparent in their accounts. The history of the Isles of Britain is one of the victims of this phenomenon. The history of Druidic lore and witchcraft are two traditions that were recorded with more than a little prejudice and often differ dramatically from the much older oral traditions of both. In accepting that there was no form of written word used on the British Isles before the arrival of the Romans, we cannot expect, and do not have, any form of written history of the ancient population of Britain; our entire understanding of our forebearers depends upon the interpretation of relatively modern-day scientific thought, which has often been proven wrong and slowly corrected.

In recent years, the significance of oral tradition has been much more recognized, and a new wave of research into oral history has burgeoned. The "pots not people" theory has turned much of the accepted history of Celtic Britain on its head, suggesting that the British Isles have never experienced a wholesale invasion of people who spoke the proto-Celtic language, the people we erroneously call the Celts, even though they only ever referred to themselves as Gaels. What the islands actually experienced was a cultural invasion that included the art, religion, and other influences of the people of Northern Europe, which produced archaeological evidence suggesting that the new pottery of the Iron Age Celt replaced the existing pottery of the indigenous Grooved ware people throughout Ireland and Wales. Current understanding is that, yes, the pottery and decoration may have influenced the indigenous people, but mitochondrial DNA evidence shows that less than 0.01 percent of the existing population of Ireland has any common ancestors with the Gaelic population of Northern Europe. In fact, linguists may argue that there is not and never has been a Celtic race; there may indeed have been a loose grouping of people who spoke a common language known as proto-Celtic, a transitory language from which developed the diverse languages of the British Isles, but these peoples never constituted a specific, definitive race or culture.

The whole point of this discussion is that we should not look at Druidic flower magic as being a Celtic practice when it is a much older and much more profound form of natural magic, well established long before the arrival of the Celtic influence. The fact that it has been retained by an oral tradition does nothing to deflect from its effectiveness or its relevance in today's society. On the contrary, the same existent oral tradition enables us to continue the practice and ensure it survives for the generations that follow us.

This continuous, unbroken tradition of flower magic is as relevant in today's world as it was for the world of our ancient ancestors. Accessing the spiritual and magical essences contained within flowers is a hugely important resource for anyone and everyone involving themselves in natural magic in any of its manifestations. We have seen that it plays a prominent role in Druidic lore, traditional witchcraft, and many other native belief systems where flowers are used in a bewildering array of practices, where we see their essential energies used in gentle, benevolent workings along with more powerful, sometimes malevolent practices. It would be a mistake to underestimate the potency of flower magic simply by virtue of the flower's delicate and enchanting appearance. Each fragile flower is imbued with the potential to facilitate unimaginable change; each subtle bloom is infused with the immense power of nature, a powerful asset available to any who choose to embrace it in the correct manner.

Index

Page references in *italics* refer to illustrations.
Numbers in *italics* preceded by *pl.* refer to color insert plate numbers.